Lifelines

Book 1

John Foster

COLLINS EDUCATIONAL

Introduction

Lifelines is a series of five books providing a course in social and personal development for all 11- to 17-year olds. The books have been designed to meet the needs of students from the first to sixth forms, and the structure is sufficiently flexible to allow teachers to use the sections selectively. The books can, therefore, easily be used with a school's own social education course in whatever way individual teachers think best.

Each book deals with a number of carefully selected topics, each divided into a series of double-page units. Each unit provides enough material for a weekly social education session. The activities are carefully structured so that individual work, pair work and group work can easily lead into or be developed out of whole class discussions. The approach is active — learning by doing and discussing — and the activities are designed so that they can take place in an ordinary classroom.

Each unit contains specific suggestions for individual follow-up activities, so that a folder of work can be built up. A number of the units provide individuals with the opportunity to reflect on their progress and thus to take more responsibility for their own learning. These units act as an on-going form of personal recording and self-assessment. They can be used in conjunction with whatever scheme for recording personal progress and achievement a school is developing.

John L. Foster, Oxford 1986

Acknowledgements

The following publishers, authors and agents are thanked for permission to reproduce extracts and copyright material:
Why Didn't They Tell the Horses? by Christine McKenna, Puffin Books (page 2); *Cannily, Cannily* by Simon French, Angus and Robertson (page 4); quotes from *Tales Out of School* by White and Brockington, Routledge and Kegan Paul (page 7); *Stars and Stripes*, 24 February 1985 (page 9); *The Oxford Journal*, 7 February 1985 (page 10); *The Street of the Starving Cats* by Margaret Fox, Hambleside Publishers (page 11); 'Jumbo and the Tin' by Tony Parker, BBC Schools TV series *WALRUS* (pages 12 and 13); information from leaflets and project kit, Royal Society For The Prevention Of Cruelty To Animals, Causeway, Horsham, Sussex RH12 1HG (details of Junior Membership and publications supplied on request to the RSPCA) (pages 14 and 15); Jane Messenger and Judy Basford (page 16); *Right!* by David Williams, first broadcast by the BBC in 1984 (page 22); *Dancing in the Streets* by Clifford Hanley, Century Hutchinson (page 23); Mick Gowar from *So Far So Good*, Collins Publishers (page 24); *Diddakoi* by Rumer Godden, Macmillan, London and Basingstoke (pages 25–26); *Jigsaw: Children of the Mountains*, the Youth and Education Department, Oxfam (page 29); chart adapted from *Project Handbook, a Guide to Student Research* by the Foundation Year Shared Time Team, Bridgewater Hall, Stantonbury Campus, Milton Keynes (page 32); adapted from chart by Sylvia Stagg and Sarah Brew, Sevenoaks School (page 35); chart compiled by Reading and Language Information Centre, University of Reading, School of Education, London Road, Reading RG1 5AQ (pages 36–37); Jimi Rand, MBA Literary Agents Ltd (page 38); extract by Daniel Freedman from 'Me, Myself, I', *Ideas in English* series, ed. Chas White and Christine Shepherd, Mary Glasgow Publications, London 1985 (page 40); quotes from *Our Names, Our Selves* by Mary Lessiter, Heinemann Books (page 42); *Computers in Everyday Life* by Ian Litterick and Chris Smithers, Wayland Publishers (page 46); *Times Educational Supplement*, 18 July 1975 (page 49); *Keep it Clean* pamphlets by the Health Education Council (page 53); 'The Blue Code' for Water Safety, Royal Life Saving Society (pages 58–59).

Photographs

Sally and Richard Greenhill pages 5, 25, 28 (right), 31; RSPCA page 14; BBC Hulton Picture Library pages 28 (left, top and bottom), 38; Brian and Sally Shuel page 31; Science Photo Library page 39; Vinnie Zuffante, Star File, Pictorial Press page 45; Information Awareness Technology Programme and Aids to Communication in Education page 48.

Artwork by Sands Straker Studios Ltd

Cartoons by Kate Shannon

Illustrations pages 12, 13, 23, 27 by Annabel Large; pages 3, 15, 19 by Annette Olney

Cover photograph courtesy of Sally and Richard Greenhill

First published 1986
Reprinted 1986, 1987 (twice)

ISBN 0 00 327435 7

Typeset by CG Graphics
Printed and bound in Great Britain by Scotprint Ltd, Musselburgh

Contents

Unit 1 | New Faces, New Places

First Time, Worst Time

It's natural to be nervous

The actress Christine McKenna loves horses. She grew up in Glasgow, so she wasn't able to learn to ride as a child. It wasn't until she landed the star role in the TV series *Flambards* that she learned to ride. The first time she went for a riding lesson she was extremely nervous.

She asked me if I had tacked up the horse. I looked at her bemusedly. 'Tacks?' Weren't they the things you use to pin up posters! What on earth could you do with them on a horse? She promptly handed me the bridle and sent me off towards the horse-box where my mount was stabled.

He was the largest, most frightening thing I'd ever seen in my life. His name was Jasper. The side of the water bucket was gripped firmly between his teeth. He was making a terrible din, bashing it against the wall. I now know this is called wind-sucking, but to my eyes here was a dragon (it couldn't possibly be a mere horse), and it was obvious that it intended to bash me to death with a wet iron bucket! I fled, but was stopped at the door by Sue who strode over to the 'dragon', lifted its head up, smacked it firmly, and told it to 'Stand up!' I gasped in admiration.

A SITUATIONS	B REASON FOR FEELING NERVOUS
Going to the dentist	Fear of being left out
Playing in a team for the first time	Fear of failure
Starting a new activity e.g. skating, gymnastics	Fear of making a fool of yourself
Taking a test or exam	Fear of pain
Going to a party	Fear of letting other people or your parents down
Going to visit friends of your parents	Fear of not knowing what to do

In pairs

1 Look at the situations listed in column A and the reasons for feeling nervous listed in column B. Talk about each situation in turn and then write down which you think is the most important reason for feeling nervous in each situation.

2 When you go away from home for the first time, it is natural to feel a little homesick. Tell one another about times when you have felt homesick. What is the best way to cope with feeling homesick? Write down a few ideas and then discuss them with other people.

The time I felt really nervous

I was excited about going on a plane, but I was worried in case I'd do something wrong at the airport.

The time I felt really nervous was when we had this test. I was frightened I'd fail.

The first time I went to stay with my cousins, I was very nervous. I was worried they wouldn't be there to meet me at the station. I didn't know what I'd do if they weren't there.

The first time I was picked for the team I was ever so nervous. I thought I might let everyone else in the team down.

When I had to go into hospital, I was dreading it, even though it was only for one night.

Class discussion

Have you ever had to go into hospital? Before going into hospital, what were the things that worried you?
Was being in hospital better or worse than you thought it would be?

Have you ever been worried because you had to make a journey on your own?
What happened on the journey? Did anything go wrong? When you actually made the journey, was it any easier or harder than you thought it would be?

Have you ever felt nervous because you were going away from home — perhaps to stay with friends or relatives? Why did you feel nervous? Did you enjoy the visit more or less than you expected?

FOR YOUR FOLDER

Think about a time when you felt really nervous. Write a few sentences about what you were going to do and why you were feeling nervous. Did things turn out better or worse than you thought they would? What do you feel about the experience now?

Being a Newcomer

Changing schools

<table>
<tr><td colspan="6">CLASS SURVEY
Aim of survey: To find out how often members of the class have changed schools before starting secondary school.

Class surveyed: 1W</td></tr>
<tr><td></td><td>Never</td><td>Once</td><td>Twice</td><td>Three times</td><td>More than three times</td></tr>
<tr><td>Aldridge, Adrian</td><td>X</td><td></td><td></td><td></td><td></td></tr>
<tr><td>Arrigo, Geraldo</td><td></td><td></td><td>X</td><td></td><td></td></tr>
<tr><td>Beesley, Sally</td><td></td><td>X</td><td></td><td></td><td></td></tr>
<tr><td>Broadbent, John</td><td>X</td><td></td><td></td><td></td><td></td></tr>
<tr><td>Cadel, Janice</td><td></td><td></td><td></td><td></td><td>X</td></tr>
<tr><td>Canning, Anita</td><td>X</td><td></td><td></td><td></td><td></td></tr>
<tr><td>Cox, Tracy</td><td></td><td>X</td><td></td><td></td><td></td></tr>
<tr><td>Dhanjal, Mohammed</td><td>X</td><td></td><td></td><td></td><td></td></tr>
<tr><td>Dingle, Simon</td><td>X</td><td></td><td></td><td></td><td></td></tr>
<tr><td>Edwards, Jennifer</td><td></td><td></td><td></td><td>X</td><td></td></tr>
<tr><td>Excell, Norton</td><td>X</td><td></td><td></td><td></td><td></td></tr>
<tr><td>Frith, Tracy</td><td>X</td><td></td><td></td><td></td><td></td></tr>
<tr><td>Giedroyc, Michael</td><td></td><td>X</td><td></td><td></td><td></td></tr>
<tr><td>Grylls, Peter</td><td></td><td></td><td></td><td></td><td>X</td></tr>
<tr><td>Hewitt, Winston</td><td></td><td></td><td>X</td><td></td><td></td></tr>
<tr><td>Jones, William</td><td>X</td><td></td><td></td><td></td><td></td></tr>
<tr><td>Knezevic, Marina</td><td>X</td><td></td><td></td><td></td><td></td></tr>
<tr><td>Ling, Earl</td><td>X</td><td></td><td></td><td></td><td></td></tr>
<tr><td>McIntosh, Fiona</td><td></td><td></td><td></td><td>X</td><td></td></tr>
<tr><td>O'Sullivan, Patricia</td><td>X</td><td></td><td></td><td></td><td></td></tr>
<tr><td>Patel, Lina</td><td>X</td><td></td><td></td><td></td><td></td></tr>
<tr><td>Pieri, Nadine</td><td></td><td></td><td>X</td><td></td><td></td></tr>
<tr><td>Rotheram, Grace</td><td>X</td><td></td><td></td><td></td><td></td></tr>
<tr><td>Ruiz, Stefan</td><td>X</td><td></td><td></td><td></td><td></td></tr>
<tr><td>Smith, James</td><td>X</td><td></td><td></td><td></td><td></td></tr>
<tr><td>Stagg, Lester</td><td></td><td>X</td><td></td><td></td><td></td></tr>
<tr><td>Todd, Christine</td><td></td><td>X</td><td></td><td></td><td></td></tr>
<tr><td>Webb, Janet</td><td></td><td></td><td>X</td><td></td><td></td></tr>
</table>

Class discussion

How many of you have had to change schools before?
Carry out a survey like 1W's and write the results on a wallchart.
Have the members of your class changed schools more or less often than the members of 1W?

The new kid

The boy in this story lives in Australia. He has changed schools often, because his parents are always on the move. He is used to having to make new friends and to fitting into new places. But it is not always easy.

He walked slowly inside. The hum of conversation abruptly stopped, and fleetingly he saw the groups of faces turned towards his own. He switched his gaze to the floorboards and stood motionless next to the doorway, the soccer ball in one hand, the shoulderbag in the other. Twenty or more of them, boys and girls with sharp country faces, sat frozen behind their desks, watching him in silence.

Trevor was acutely aware of the sea of eyes fixed on him and vainly tried to focus his mind elsewhere. The teacher still hadn't entered the room, and slowly the hum of conversation resumed.

'Hey, mate,' said a voice, 'how old are you?'

'He's pretty small.'

Ripples of laughter. Trevor remained silent.

'Reckon you're in the wrong class, mate. Kindergarten's the other side of the playground.'

More laughter.

'Jeez, he's quiet. Say something.'

'What's the soccer ball for?'

'You got hair like a girl, mate.'

'Maybe he is . . .'

The talk stopped as the teacher walked into the room.

1 What do you think of the way the class treated Trevor?

2 How did Trevor behave? What must he have been feeling?
If you were Trevor and faced with the same situation, what would you do?

3 Suggest why Trevor took the football to school with him.
Do you think it is a good idea to take something special to school with you on your first day as a newcomer?

4 What is the worst thing about being a newcomer?
What is the best thing about being a newcomer?

Joining in

In groups

Role-play
A group is playing a game in the playground when a newcomer arrives. The newcomer stands and watches, then asks to join in.

1   Plan and then act out a scene in which the newcomer is at first ignored and then told to go away.

2   Plan and then act out a scene in which the group stop playing, gather round the newcomer, ask some questions and then invite the newcomer to join in.

Repeat the scenes a number of times with different people playing the part of the newcomer.

Class discussion

Talk about how the people who played the newcomer felt a) when they were left out, and b) when they were invited to join in.

● What makes you decide whether to let a newcomer join in?

● Does it depend mainly on a) the mood of the group, or b) what the leader says?

● Is it right to make decisions about a person based on how the person a) looks, b) talks, and c) acts?

● Should you let what you have heard about a person influence your decision?

Starting Secondary School

What should I do?

Can you help these first years to solve their problems?

In groups

Talk about the situations shown above.
If the children were at your school, what exactly should they do?
Choose someone to act as a reporter for your group. Get the reporter to write down what the group thinks the person with the problem should do in each case. When you have finished, hold a class discussion. Compare the advice that your group gives with the advice given by other groups.

First fortnight

Here are some extracts written by older children. They are writing about how they felt when they started at secondary school.

I didn't look forward to going. The one I went to had a bad reputation; all the lads who went there were supposed to be bullies, and me and my mates were really worried about going. It seemed massive compared to the other school. Primary school was about ten classrooms, but this one had fifty or sixty rooms. There were thousands of pupils compared to the two hundred at primary school. I felt lonely.

Primary school was like a little community. Secondary school seemed so large. But it was better than I'd thought it would be.

Robert

It's scary for the first week. I thought I'd be with my friends from middle school but we were split up. When you get to know people and you get to know teachers, it's great because you find a whole new circle of friends, so you've got your friends at home as well as school.

Prakash

I felt grown-up moving from primary to secondary, but I was very nervous. In fact, I fainted on my first day. It was very hot and I had my new uniform on. We were being welcomed by the headmistress and everything went fuzzy.

Audrey

FOR YOUR FOLDER

My first fortnight

Remember your first fortnight at secondary school. Here are some questions for you to think about:

What did you look forward to about starting secondary school?

What were you worried about?

Have there been any things which you have found 'scary'?

Have you made any mistakes that have upset you?

Has anything pleased you because it has gone very well?

Is there anything that you are still particularly worried about?

What do you think you achieved during your first fortnight at secondary school?

Write a few sentences saying how you feel about your first fortnight at secondary school.

Codes of Behaviour

Behind the rules

```
                    LABORATORY CODE

ENTERING THE LAB
● You may only go into the Lab if a teacher is
  there.
● Before lessons wait quietly outside until told to go
  in.
● Never run in the Lab.

APPARATUS
● Do not touch any laboratory apparatus, taps or
  switches, unless told to do so.
● Only use apparatus for the purpose instructed by
  the teacher.
● If you break anything tell the teacher AT ONCE.

USING CHEMICALS
● ALWAYS read the label on the bottle to make sure
  that you have the right one.
● Pour from bottles, with your hand around the
  label.
● Once you have taken chemicals away, NEVER put
  them back into the bottle.
● Never mix any chemicals until you are told to do
  so.
● WEAR safety spectacles when using chemicals.
● Never taste or sniff anything in the lab unless
  your teacher tells you to.
● When heating chemicals, always point the mouth
  of the test tube away from other people and
  yourself.
● Always wipe your bench clean if you spill
  anything.

ACCIDENTS
● If an accident happens KEEP CALM and tell your
  teacher AT ONCE, then do exactly as you are told.

FIRE
● If your experiment catches fire WALK QUIETLY
  away from it, and call your teacher. NEVER try to
  put it out yourself.

SINKS
● Do not drop paper of any kind into the sink.
● Never attempt to wash solids, however small,
  down the drain.

HOT APPARATUS
● ALWAYS ask your teacher before putting away hot
  apparatus, e.g. tripods and gauzes.
```

In groups

1 Study the laboratory code. Explain to each other the reasons for each of the rules. Are there any that you don't understand?

2 Here is a list of some of the things people do wrong at school:

> Smoking in the toilets
> Being cheeky to a teacher
> Scribbling on a textbook
> Cheating in a test
> Arriving at school late
> Fighting in the playground
> Stealing from someone's bag
> Bringing bottles to school
> Failing to do homework on time
> Leaving the premises without permission

Draw two columns on a piece of paper. Label the columns *A. Offence, B. Punishment.*
In the first column, list the things people do wrong at school, numbering them 1 to 10. Start with the offence which you consider to be the most serious, e.g. if you think stealing is the most serious, then write down 1. Stealing from someone's bag.
In the second column, write down what you think the punishment for that offence should be.
Compare your lists with those of other groups.

FOR YOUR FOLDER

1 Look at a copy of your school rules. Go through the rules one by one. Suggest the reasons for each rule and say what will happen to you in each case if you break that rule.
2 Here is a list of different types of punishment. Write a few sentences, saying which of them you think is the most effective and why.
Lunch-time detention, lines, after-school detention, extra work, a letter to your parents, picking up litter, withdrawal of privileges, on report.
3 Are there any rules you feel should be added to the list?

Suspended boys made to walk to school

In Conway, Arkansas two school-boys, Harry aged eleven and his brother David aged nine, have been suspended from using the school bus for five days, because of their rowdy behaviour on the bus. While they are suspended, their parents are refusing to take them to school by car. So the two boys have to leave home at 6.30 a.m. to start a seven mile walk in order to get to school in time for an 8.30 a.m. start. After school, they face another two-hour walk home.

On one of the days, nine-year-old David was picked up by a police officer who spotted him walking along the side of a four-lane high-way. The police officer gave him a lift and dropped him near his home. When David's parents found out that he had accepted a ride, he was punished for doing so.

The boys were suspended after they had received two warnings for constantly being out of their seats. Their mother said: 'Smacking them didn't help. Grounding them didn't help. Taking away their toys didn't help. This is the only thing we can think of to do. We want them to understand that they caused this and they have to face up to the conse-quences.'

The principal of Conway Middle School commented: 'We're responsi-ble for them on the school bus and suspending them for five days was the only way we felt we could handle the situation. We've talked with the parents, but they feel that if they drive them to school they would be condoning their behaviour.'

In groups

- Do you think the boys' parents were right to refuse to drive them to school?

- Do you think they were right to make the boys walk to school?

- Would it have been better a) to have kept the boys at home all day and made them do schoolwork, or b) to have sent them to school by public transport?

- Was it wrong of David to accept a lift from the police officer? Did he deserve to be punished for doing so?

- If you were the boys' parents, how would you have dealt with the situation?

- What would you have said to the boys to make them realise that they must behave on the bus? What punishment, if any, would you have given them in addition to the suspension?

Report back to the class with your group findings.

FOR YOUR FOLDER

Work in pairs. Draw up a code of behaviour for pupils who use the school bus. In addition to saying how pupils are expected to behave when they are on the bus, include instructions about how they are expected to behave while they are waiting for the bus and while they are getting on and off. Decide what action will be taken to deal with someone who repeatedly fails to follow the code. When you have finished, each make a copy of the code of behaviour for your folder.

Harmless or Harmful?

Staying out

Alexis sleeps in a ditch while police comb county

OXFORDSHIRE'S very own Just William has done it again.

Little terror Alexis Holden ran away from home and spent the night in a ditch . . . as police combed the county with tracker dogs and helicopters.

They scoured lonely lanes and remote farm buildings, while 12-year-old Alexis wrapped himself snugly in a blanket and watched the trains go by his hiding place.

Absolute hell

It wasn't until late the next morning that he was discovered calmly visiting a friend in Charlbury, six miles away from the pretty cottage in Sarsgrove, near Chipping Norton, where he lives with his parents and four brothers and sisters.

'My husband Nick and I went through absolute hell,' said Alexis's mum Janet.

'We were praying he'd been sensible, and not let himself be picked up by some strange man.

'He'd run away before, at Christmas 1980, and spent the night in a hollow tree-trunk. This time he got

into hot water because he had a row with his young brother, George, on the way home from Chipping Norton School on Friday.

'He's got a pretty fiery temper, and he stormed out of the house. I thought he'd just gone to cool off . . . but when he wasn't back by 7.30, three hours later, I got worried and phoned the police.'

Janet and Nick, a 39-year-old window cleaner, didn't sleep a wink that night.

'I kept waiting for the knock on the door, and a policeman saying Alexis had been found dead in a ditch,' said Janet.

'And that's where he was . . . but safe, thank God.

'It wasn't until two next afternoon that the police brought him home.

Shattered

'He'd been found at the home of his classmate Shane Clifton, in Charlbury.

'He was absolutely shattered when he got home. We put him straight to bed. We were too relieved to be angry with him.'

Alexis, wearing a cheeky grin reminiscent of children's book hero Just William, said: 'It was great. I'd taken my own blanket, and I found a dry ditch near Charlbury railway station. So I curled up nice and snug and watched the trains. I had no idea the police were looking for me.'

Now police plan to visit Alexis . . for 'a stern talking-to.'

Here are some views of what Alexis did:

> RUNNING OFF LIKE THAT DOESN'T SOLVE ANYTHING. IT ONLY CREATES MORE PROBLEMS, NOT ONLY FOR HIM AND HIS FAMILY BUT ALSO FOR PEOPLE LIKE THE POLICE.

> His behaviour was selfish, immature and inconsiderate.

> I DON'T SEE WHAT ALL THE FUSS WAS ABOUT. IF HE WANTS TO GO OFF ON HIS OWN IT'S UP TO HIM.

> I admire him for going off on his own like that. It takes a lot of courage.

In groups

- What does your group think of what Alexis did? Which of the views do you agree with?

- Do you think Alexis deserved to be punished? If you were his parents would you have punished him and if so, how?

- What do you think the police officer will say to Alexis when he gives him a stern talking to? List the things you would say to Alexis if you were the police officer.

- What does the reporter think of Alexis's behaviour? Does he approve or disapprove of it? Does writing a newspaper story about Alexis make him into more of a hero than he deserves to be?

- How do the views of each of the groups differ? One person from each group should tell the rest of the class what the *majority* verdict on Alexis's behaviour was: selfish, harmless, courageous, immature, understandable, etc.

A game of dare

After a while Marty grew bored with the High Street. 'What you say to a game of dare?' he asked the gang. They fell in with the idea joyfully so he led them away from the shops and up the hill past the Bingo Hall. When they came alongside the railway line the gang followed him through a gap in the railings and up a steep bank. Atlee could hear the trains rattling along the track above their heads. From the top of the embankment there was a clear view of the amazing crisscross of lines which led to the Junction. Atlee stood, spellbound by the scene which was unlike anything he had ever seen before. He had never imagined there could be so many lines in the whole world, let alone in one place. Two trains passed close to where he stood and he started back in fright. The gang laughed. Marty began to lead him towards the track.

'You can have first go because you're new,' he told Atlee.

Atlee was puzzled. 'First go, first go at what?'

'Dare, of course. When a train comes you see who dares to wait longest to cross the track, you can go first 'cos you're new. Doin' you a favour, see.'

Another train snaked its way over the points on its way to the Junction. Although it was obviously slowing down as it approached it was still moving at a fair speed. Atlee did not like the sound of this game at all. 'That's dangerous ain't it?' he asked.

The gang laughed nastily. 'You chicken?' asked Marty. Atlee shook his head, he did not want to appear a coward.

There was a distant rattle up the line. 'Train coming, get ready,' yelled Marty. From a faint grey shape in the distance, grew a huge, yellow locomotive, beating its way down the fast line.

'It's a fast,' shouted Marty, 'you'll have to be slippy.' He grabbed Atlee's arm and pulled him towards the fast line. They could feel the vibrations running along the track as the train approached. Atlee's heart beat like a sledge-hammer inside his chest, in time with the pounding wheels.

Marty pushed Atlee forward, 'Now!'

Atlee looked up as he went forward. He caught sight of the horror-stricken face of the train driver looking down on him from the cab and knew it was too late. Too late!

A great rush of air hit Atlee and he felt himself being sucked in towards the train's racing wheels. He threw himself face down on the ground by the track. Roaring and clanking, the train thundered past.

It was not until the last carriage had cleared the section and was well on its way to the Junction that Atlee dared to lift his head. Marty, Mike and the gang were watching him from a safe distance, part way down the bank. Only their heads were visible to Atlee.

'Coward!' yelled Marty.

'Coward!' yelled Mike.

'Coward!' yelled the gang.

They rolled down the bank and were gone.

Atlee shakily pulled himself to his feet, wiping dust out of his eyes. A man was running towards him, waving his arms and shouting. Atlee did not wait to hear what the man wanted but scrambled down the bank and made for the street. Stumbling and crying with fright, he found his way back to the Junction and up the hill, on the opposite side, to his own street.

In groups

- What do you think of the way Marty treats Atlee?

- Is Atlee 'a coward'?

- Discuss the view that it is more cowardly of the gang to scare Atlee than it is of Atlee to be scared of crossing the track.

- Tell each other about games of dare in which you have been involved.

Report back to the class with your group findings.

FOR YOUR FOLDER

The leader of a group of children suggests a game of dare that will involve doing something dangerous. Although most of the children are apprehensive about joining in because of the danger, they agree to do so because they don't want to be called 'chicken'. One of them refuses to join in and there is an argument between her/him and the leader. Write down this argument in the form of a short playscript.

Honesty Pays?

Finders keepers...

DAD *is sitting at one end of the kitchen table finishing off hamburger, egg, beans and chips. MUM is sitting at the other end of the table drinking a mug of coffee and looking at The Sun. ERIC, aged 16, is sitting on one side of the table. He has finished eating and is reading a comic. RONNIE, aged 13, is on the other side of the table.*

DAD: (*Looking at RONNIE*) Close your eyes.
RONNIE: Eh? What for?
DAD: Go on. I said close your eyes.
(*RONNIE closes his eyes. DAD leans across the table. He puts a gold ballpoint pen with a digital timepiece in the side in front of RONNIE*)
DAD: Right, you can open them again now.
RONNIE: Cor!
ERIC: (*Not showing much interest*) Where'd you get that?
DAD: Found it — in some grass on that bit of old ground where the petrol pumps used to be.
MUM: (*Mildly, not showing much interest*) Someone's probably lost it, you ought to hand it in.
DAD: Oh yeah, where? At the police station? That'd be the last *anyone* saw of it, that would, wouldn't it!
MUM: It might be valuable. Somebody might be looking for it.

DAD: Well, if it was valuable, they ought to have looked after it better, shouldn't they, eh? (*He grins as he remembers something he and his mates used to say when he was at school*) 'Finders keepers, losers weepers' eh? (*He turns to RONNIE*) Well, d'you want it?
RONNIE: Ooh, yes please Dad. Yeh!
DAD: Well, go on then, take it. Before I change me mind and do what your Mum says.
RONNIE: Cor, thanks, ta!
(*RONNIE picks up the pen and starts to inspect it*)

In groups

Choose a reporter to note down the opinions of the group on each of the questions below.

1 'Finders keepers, losers weepers.' What do you think of this view?

2 Would it have made a difference if:
a) a friend of Dad's had said he'd found the pen and given it to him?
b) it had been an ordinary pen, without a digital timepiece?

3 Here are two other people's views:

> It's my pen. I lost it. He should have handed it in. If he keeps it, he's stealing it.

The owner of the pen

> We get a lot of people coming in about things they've lost. Some of them are very upset. If you find anything at all, you should hand it in.

A police office

Think about the incident from the owner's point of view. Would it have made a difference to your views if it had been *your* pen?

Class discussion

The reporter for each group should *summarise*, for the rest of the class, his or her group's views on each question.

12

Losers weepers

RONNIE *is on his way home from school one day when he finds a tin hidden under some stones. When he opens the tin, he finds £500 inside. He and his friends talk about what they should do, but they cannot agree.*

LARRY: I don't want a share if you share it out. I don't want anything to do with it. I still say what I said last week — put it back.

TITCH: I think you ought to take it to the police and tell them where you found it. They'll know if it's been stolen or not.

ALICE: I know what. Why don't we ask one of the teachers — Mr Jatti — he's sensible. He'd know what was the best thing.

RONNIE: Listen — let's do what I said in the first place. Divide it up between us. We all take our share and spend it or whatever we like, and then forget about it.

In pairs

Decide what you think the children should do. Should they:
a) share it out?
b) hand it to the police?
c) ask a grown-up for advice?
d) put it back?
Write your choice on a piece of paper.

Would it make a difference if:
a) the amount of money was not so large?
b) the money had not obviously been hidden?
c) the children knew someone who had definitely lost the money?
Write your answer to each question on the same piece of paper.

Class discussion

By a show of hands, or by taking in the pieces of paper, find out what most of the pairs thought the children should do. Was one course of action more popular than the others and, if so, why?

What about the other questions? Did most of the pairs have the same opinions? If not, why not?

In pairs

Role play
Act out these scenes.
'That's mine!' Two children argue over an object, such as a bracelet or a coin. One is the person who lost it. The other is the person who found it.

'Where did you find it?' A scene at a police station, when a girl or boy hands in an object she or he has found. The police officer asks for full details of where it was found and thanks the girl or boy for handing it in.

FOR YOUR FOLDER

Work in pairs. Four children find a wallet. It contains £2. There is also a slip of paper in it which gives the name and address of the owner. The children know the man and don't like him. Two of the group think they should return the wallet to the owner. The third thinks they should take it to the police station. The fourth says they should divide the money between them.
Write out the argument in the form of a short script. Copy it into your folder.

Who Cares About Pets?

Pets and their needs

Your pet's basic needs are simple. It needs regular food and water, but feeding costs do not have to be too high. Dogs require a balanced mixture of protein, in the form of tinned meat or fresh cheap cuts, and carbohydrate in the form of biscuit, meal or bread. Cats require a high protein diet, but you do not have to buy the highest quality meat or fish for them. Dogs need exercise every day if they are to remain healthy and lively, and cats and smaller animals need access to the outdoors.

Animals respond well to training, so train your dog not to jump up, to walk properly on a lead and to come when called. As well as making sure it is house-trained, it can also be trained not to mess the pavement and to use only a certain part of the garden as easily as to sit on command.

Grooming and cleaning is a process which all animals enjoy, and long-haired animals need. It is occasionally necessary to deal with fleas. Proper veterinary care is essential for all animals as pets are as likely to fall ill or to have accidents as humans are, and if they are unwell or in pain, then they need professional attention. During the first few months of their lives, dogs should be vaccinated against certain diseases and cats can be vaccinated against some diseases too. Worming is also essential early in life for both cats and dogs.

Human company is vital to the well-being of pets – dogs in particular. Don't leave your dog on its own for long periods of time. Thousands of pets live lonely, boring and monotonous lives without their owners giving them so much as a thought. A rabbit, in his small hutch, attempts to relieve the monotony of his lonely existence by overturning his food and water pots, a chained dog trying to get its freedom barks incessantly; these are just two common examples of everyday boredom in pet animals, which could easily be overcome by a more thoughtful, caring owner.

FOR YOUR FOLDER

1 Looking after a pet properly takes time and costs money. Choose one of the pets from this list: cat, dog, rabbit, pony, gerbil, hamster, budgerigar.
a) Make a list of all the jobs you must do each week in order to care for your pet properly. Beside each activity, write down the time it takes

e.g. Buying pet food   30 minutes
Cleaning cage   10 minutes a day = 70 minutes per week

Work out how much time you have to spend each day caring for your pet's needs.
b) List all the expenses you have each week in order to meet your pet's needs. Then, list the extra expenses you might need to budget for during a year, e.g. vet's fees, boarding kennels. Work out how much money you think it would cost to keep your pet each year.

Unwanted pets – a growing problem

Britain's domestic animal population is out of control. Every year the number of unwanted and abandoned pets increases. Every year local councils, vets and organisations like the RSPCA have no option but to destroy hundreds of thousands of animals. Soon, the time may come when we need to have laws restricting the ownership of pets. If we want to stop that happening, says the RSPCA, then we must take action now.

WHY DO PEOPLE KEEP PETS?

Animals — particularly domestic animals — have always played a part in traditional British family life. Dogs are by far the most popular pets, with an estimated 5½ million owned in Great Britain. Cats are not as numerous, but have increased in popularity in recent years.

People keep pets because they're fun to have around. Anybody who has ever enjoyed the company of a pet knows well enough just how strong the bond between human and animal can be. Elderly or lonely people often depend on a pet for their only company. In certain circumstances, pets can help people who have been ill. Doctors have proved that a pet can play a part in helping someone to recover from a mental or physical disease. Keeping a pet can help children to learn the meaning of loyalty, unselfishness and friendship.

BUT the commitment to a pet doesn't begin and end with a visit to the local pet shop. It's a commitment for the whole of that animal's lifetime — anything up to twenty years of total responsibility for its health and well-being.

The sad truth is that in too many cases the present of a pet to a child goes wrong. Both the child and the parents find that looking after the pet is too much trouble. The pet is either abandoned or neglected.

One of the busiest times of the year for the RSPCA is always six months after Christmas. This is the time when people have to think about getting a dog licence for the puppy they bought at Christmas. It is also summer holiday time and they just can't be bothered to put it in a kennel or to find someone to look after it while they go away.

It is a sad state of affairs. What is needed, says the RSPCA, is for the public to change its attitude towards animals. Having a pet involves time, money and patience. So anyone thinking of getting a pet should stop and think: **Am I willing to accept the responsibility that keeping a pet involves?**

STRAY AND UNWANTED DOGS ARE A PUBLIC NUISANCE. THERE SHOULD BE A HIGHER LICENCE FEE, WHICH COULD PAY FOR A SYSTEM OF DOG WARDENS.

Group discussion

A 73-year-old widow said she planned to leave instructions in her will for her three pets — two dogs aged 8 and 13 and a cat aged 15 — to be destroyed after her death.

It's the kindest thing for them. All would have the greatest difficulty at their age adjusting to new owners and strange surroundings.

What do you think of her plans? Are they cruel or just realistic?

Discuss this view. Should the cost of the dog licence be increased? What powers would you give to dog wardens?

When you have discussed these questions in groups, share your views with the rest of the class.

In pairs

Make a list of the advantages and disadvantages of keeping a dog or cat for *each* of the following people:
a) a twelve-year-old, b) a young, working mother, and c) a retired pensioner.
Remember to think about it from the point of view of both the owner *and the pet*. Compare your lists with those of other pairs.

How Responsible Are You?

How much will-power and self-discipline do you have?

Read through the following list of imaginary situations and choose which response is closest to the way in which *you* would think or act. Be honest and write down what you would actually do, rather than what you think you ought to do. When you have finished, use the quiz score sheet to work out your score.

1 You have homework to do for the following day.
Do you prefer to:
A get it done as soon as you can when you get home?
B decide to do it later and then forget about it and not have enough time to do it properly?
C not have any plan of action at all?
D decide to do it at a certain time and do it then?

2 You always have games lessons on the same day each week.
Do you:
A rely on your mother or someone to sort out your kit?
B check your kit and pack it the night before?
C leave it and try to borrow some at school?
D frantically search for it before you go to school?

3 You have to buy a present for a friend or member of your family.
Do you:
A borrow money to buy it?
B save regularly in advance for it?
C hope that some money will 'turn up' somehow?
D decide not to give a present?

4 You have been ill and missed a week's school.
Would you:
A check with your teachers to see which work you need to catch up on?
B copy notes from your friends' books, not knowing or caring whether they are correct?
C think to yourself 'I can catch up later', knowing that you probably won't?
D not give a thought to the missed work?

5 You've borrowed a cassette from a friend who wants it back. It's somewhere in your house, but you aren't really sure where.
Would you:
A forget about it until you're asked for it again?
B look for it as soon as you realise that your friend wants it?
C think to yourself that it'll probably turn up tomorrow and not worry much?
D be prepared to replace it, i.e. buy a new one?

Quiz score sheet	4 A 20	8 A 10
	B 10	B 10
1 A 20	C 5	C 5
B 10	D 0	D 20
C 5	5 A 5	9 A 10
D 15	B 20	B 20
2 A 5	C 5	C 0
B 20	D 20	D 5
C 5	6 A 0	10 A 20
D 10	B 10	B 20
3 A 10	C 20	C 5
B 20	D 5	D 5
C 10	7 A 20	11 A 20
D 5	B 0	B 5
	C 5	C 15
	D 5	D 0

Over 200 — Wonderful.
150–200 — Not bad. Keep trying for perfection.
65–150 — Room for improvement.
Under 65 — Oh dear.

In groups

a) Look at the situations opposite.
b) Try to suggest why the people concerned in each case acted as they did.
c) What are the consequences of each situation for the people involved?

6 If you were told that there were important tests in six weeks' time, would you:
A think that you know it all and that it is a waste of time to go through your books?
B plan to revise regularly, start off well and then abandon your plan?
C plan a revision timetable allowing a certain amount of time for each subject on a regular basis, and keep to it?
D think that you have loads of time and then forget about the tests until the week or even the night before and then work in a panic?

7 You have been told a very interesting secret and have been asked *not* to tell anyone else.
Would you:
A not mention it to a single person?
B think that it is too interesting to keep to yourself and tell everyone you can think of?
C just tell your one reliable friend and swear him/her to secrecy?
D blurt it out without thinking in front of several people?

8 You want a pet and promise to look after it if you can have one. From past experience and knowledge of your own character would you:
A care for it really well for a few weeks and then not bother?
B do the job well on some days but not at all on others?
C leave someone else to look after the pet when you are tired of it?
D look after it carefully and regularly for evermore even if you find it boring?

9 Your room is in so much of a mess (not necessarily your fault!) that it is hard to find what you want.
Do you:
A start tidying it and then get interested in something you've found and forget the tidying?
B tidy it up immediately?
C continue living in the mess?
D promise yourself that you will do it later, and eventually do it?

10 You are often late for school or for your bus. To put this right do you:
A set the alarm to go off 10 minutes earlier or ask to be woken up earlier?
B pack your bag and prepare everything the night before?
C go without breakfast to save time?
D think that it isn't really your fault?

11 You have agreed to play for a school team on a particular day. A friend then asks you to go on a birthday outing on that day.
Do you:
A play in the team because that was your first commitment?
B say that you can't play?
C ask the teacher if you could be excused from the team?
D just not turn up to play?

Bullying in the dinner queue — two older pupils push in front of first year pupils, elbowing them out of the way.

Some third-year boys let off a fire extinguisher in the corridor.

Going through the doors in the corridor, someone lets the door swing back and it hits a pupil in the face.

After break, people are rushing upstairs to get to the next lesson and someone falls in the rush.

Report back to the class with your group findings.

FOR YOUR FOLDER

What do *you* find hard to do or not to do? (Look again at the things mentioned in the quiz.) Suggest ways in which you can help yourself to be more self-disciplined in these matters, e.g. planning ahead, organising your time better, thinking how your actions may affect others.

Homework Matters

Finding the time

> **ERROL**: Are you going to the youth club tonight, Jace?
>
> **JASON**: Dunno. I might. It all depends.
>
> **ERROL**: Terry's going. Aren't you T?
>
> **TERRY**: Course I'm going. Go on Jace.
>
> **JASON**: Like I said. It depends.
>
> **TERRY**: What's it depend on? You haven't got to babysit have you?
>
> **JASON**: No. It depends on whether or not I get all my homework done.
>
> **ERROL**: All what homework?
>
> **JASON**: You know. That English story for Crabtree. It's got to be in tomorrow.
>
> **ERROL**: Oh, that. I've done that. That won't take you all evening. You can do that during Grange Hill.
>
> **JASON**: Have you done it already then? How?
>
> **ERROL**: Did it on the bus, didn't we T?
>
> **TERRY**: That's right. Knocked off a quick page. No trouble.
>
> **ERROL**: Come on, Jace. It won't take you more than five minutes, then you can come down the club.
>
> **JASON**: It's not just that. There's that French as well. She's going to give us a test on those words, remember?
>
> **ERROL**: Learn 'em on the bus tomorrow. Honestly, Jace, I dunno what's come over you. You're taking this whole homework business far too seriously. What I say is schoolwork's for schooltime, and if the teachers think I'm going to spend all my free time doing their schoolwork, they're wrong. That's right, isn't it T?
>
> **TERRY**: That's right, Errol.

Why do you get homework?

'It helps you to learn to work on your own. It teaches you how to plan and organise your work.'

'It gives you the chance to practise what you have done in class, or to do some background work that will help you to understand what's coming next.'

'It gives the teacher a chance to check that you have understood the lesson and to find out about any difficulties you are having.'

'It helps you to learn by thinking things out for yourself and putting them into your own words.'

Group discussion

What is the value of homework?
Before you begin, each write down on a slip of paper your answer to the question by completing this sentence: 'I think homework is valuable because. . .' After you have finished your discussion, share the views of your group with the rest of the class.

In pairs

Role play
Develop these situations. Repeat each one, so that you both have a turn at being each character.

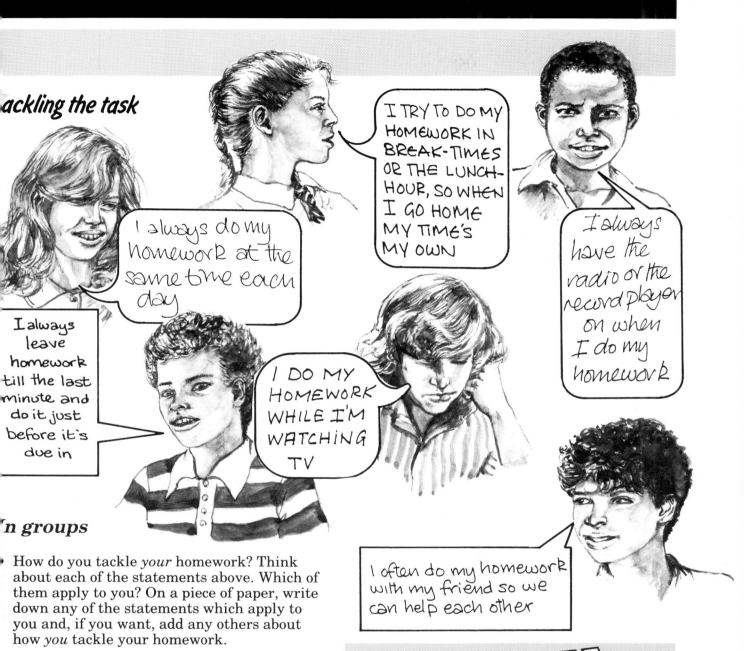

ackling the task

> I always do my homework at the same time each day

> I TRY TO DO MY HOMEWORK IN BREAK-TIMES OR THE LUNCH-HOUR, SO WHEN I GO HOME MY TIME'S MY OWN

> I always have the radio or the record player on when I do my homework

> I always leave homework till the last minute and do it just before it's due in

> I DO MY HOMEWORK WHILE I'M WATCHING TV

> I often do my homework with my friend so we can help each other

n groups

How do you tackle *your* homework? Think about each of the statements above. Which of them apply to you? On a piece of paper, write down any of the statements which apply to you and, if you want, add any others about how *you* tackle your homework.

Talk about what you have all written.

Choose a group reporter to write out what your group considers to be the *most important* points to enable you to do your homework successfully.

Class discussion

Discuss the different views that groups have on how to do successful homework. Ask your teacher to write each of the points on the blackboard and ake a vote to decide which are *the* most important.

FOR YOUR FOLDER

A friend has asked for your advice on the best way to tackle homework. Write out a list of Dos and Don'ts called 'How to do good homework'.
Here is the first piece of advice from such a list:
1 Don't leave your homework until the last minute.

Presentation Counts

In pairs

Study the two pieces of homework that are reproduced on the opposite page. Both pupils were using the same source book and both were asked to: 'Write notes on the different kinds of volcanoes'.

There is nothing factually wrong with the piece of work produced by pupil A, but pupil B has produced a much more successful piece, for two main reasons:

1   It is a much more highly organised and carefully presented piece of work, and

2   Pupil B has included many more technical terms and, wherever possible, has included examples.

Talk about the use pupil B has made of these devices: headings, numbers, capitals, underlining, brackets. Are there any other devices that you use when asked to make notes for homework?

Role play
If you were the teacher, what would you say to pupil A to try to help him improve his work? Act out a scene in which you talk to pupil A about how to present homework.

FOR YOUR FOLDER

Check up on yourself
Select a piece of homework you have done recently and use this self-assessment test, a) to see how successfully you think you did it, and b) to set yourself targets for improvement.

The appearance of your work
1   Is your work, a) very neat, b) quite neat, c) rather untidy, d) very untidy?
2   Did you rule off underneath the previous piece of work?
3   Did you leave a margin?
4   Did you put a proper title and date?
5   Were any crossings-out done neatly or untidily?
6   How neat is your handwriting? Would it help you to improve your work if you had help with your handwriting?

The content of your work
1   Did you arrange your work properly in paragraphs or sections?
2   Did you make use of any of the following: sub-headings, underlining, numbers, capitals, brackets? If not, could you have done so?
3   Did you read your work through before you handed it in, to check the spelling and punctuation?
4   How accurate and clear were any diagrams or drawings that you included?

5   Did you go over the work when you were given it back to correct any mistakes? Did you write in any important points which you had missed out?

Overall grade
If you had to grade this piece of work using a five-star system, how many stars would you give yourself for, a) its appearance, b) its content, and c) the amount of effort you put into it? (Be honest!)
★★★★★ Excellent   ★★★★ Good
★★★ Satisfactory   ★★ Poor   ★ Unsatisfactory

Targets for improvement
Set yourself targets for improvement. Write down one way in which you will try to improve the *appearance* and one way in which you will try to improve the *content* of your next piece of homework. Tell a friend what your targets for improvement are. You could also speak to your form/subject teacher about how you could improve your homework.
When you have done the homework and had it back, use the five-star system to give yourself grades for your homework. Then, show your friend the homework and say whether or not you think you managed to achieve your targets.

Volcanoes

There are many different kinds of volcanoes. Some of them are likely to blow up at any time. Others are said to be asleep, because they haven't blown up for a long time. Others have stopped blowing up altogether. Some volcanoes erupt violently. A volcano called Krakatoa blew up violently in 1883 and a lot of people died. Other volcanoes only erupt quietly. When a volcano erupts, it forms a hill called a cone. Different eruptions produce different shapes of cone. Some are pointed, others have gently sloping sides and look like shields.

eading, nderlined →

se of nderlining to aw attention technical rms →

se of b-headings, nderlined →

se of mbers to stinguish fferent points, this case fferent types cones →

26th April ← Date

Different Kinds of Volcanoes

There are three different kinds of volcanoes:

1. Volcanoes that keep on erupting. These are called active volcanoes. Example: Mount St Helens (USA) ← Use of examples

2. Volcanoes that have not erupted for a while. These are dormant volcanoes. Example: ← Space left in which to add example after asking teacher

3. Volcanoes that have stopped erupting. These are called extinct volcanoes.

KINDS OF ERUPTIONS

EXPLOSIVE eruptions. Very violent.
Example: Krakatoa (Indonesia, 1883 – 36,000 dead) ← Use of brackets in which to include additional information
QUIET eruptions. No violent explosion. Lava flows out freely.
Example: Volcanoes on Hawaii.

DIFFERENT SHAPES OF VOLCANOES

Different eruptions produce different shaped hills (CONES).

1. Explosive eruptions produce CINDER CONES. ← These are pointed and made of ash and cinders.

2. Quiet eruptions produce SHIELD VOLCANOES, with gently sloping sides made of layers of lava. ← Use of capital letters for key terms

3. Many volcanoes are COMPOSITE CONES formed by a series of quiet and explosive eruptions.
   Example: Mount Fuji (Japan – last erupted 1707.)

Picking a Fight

Why do fights start?

LES: Hey you!
TIM: Who? Me?
LES: You I'm talking to. You.
TIM: What?
LES: Who do you think you're staring at?
TIM: You what?
LES: Who do you think you're looking at?
TIM: I'm not looking at anybody.
LES: You are. You're looking at me.
TIM: I'm not.
LES: You are. You're doing it now.
TIM: Only 'cause you shouted. I wasn't looking before.
LES: You were. You were staring.
TIM: I wasn't.
LES: You were.
TIM: I wasn't.
LES: Are you calling me a liar?
TIM: No.
LES: You are.
TIM: I'm just telling you. I'm just saying, I wasn't looking at you. Honest.
LES: So you're saying I'm a liar, then.
TIM: No.
LES: You'd better watch who you're calling a liar.
TIM: I'm not.
LES: You'd better look out, that's all.
TIM: What for?
LES: For me. You'd better look out for me.
TIM: You said I hadn't to.
LES: What?
TIM: Look at you.
LES: Are you trying to be funny?
TIM: No.
LES: Don't try to be funny with me.

TIM: I wasn't. It was just a joke.
LES: You'll not be laughing when I've finished with you.
TIM: I'm not laughing. Who's laughing? I'm not.
LES: You'll be laughing on the other side of your face. You don't mess with Les.
TIM: Eh?
LES: You don't mess with Les. What are you grinning at?
TIM: I'm not. It's just the way my mouth is.
LES: Right. Down the dene after school.
TIM: Which dene?
LES: What you mean, which dene? The dene.
TIM: I don't go home that way.
LES: You'd better be there.
TIM: I've got the bus to catch.
LES: Be there!
TIM: Right!
LES: Right!

In pairs

1   Read the conversation through twice, taking it in turns to be Les and Tim. As you read the parts, try to imagine what the person is thinking and feeling, while he is speaking.

2   Talk about how Les feels while he is speaking to Tim.
a) Did Les want to pick a fight with Tim?
b) Can you think of any reasons why Les might want to fight Tim?

3   Talk about how Tim feels during the conversation and think of words to sum up his feelings, e.g. worried, angry.

4   Is a conversation like this bound to lead to a challenge to a fight?

Class discussion

Discuss the answers you've come up with while working in pairs. Then, on the blackboard, do a brainstorm on 'Why fights start'. Copy the brainstorm into your folder.

Fighting — what do you think?

To be honest, I had given up the fight-game for life, but there was a crowd of older boys who sponsored the match after this other boy had landed a stone unprovoked, on the back of my head. They wanted sport, and I felt I was armed with justice, so we squared up. I'm not even sure what the other boy's name was, but I think it was Hannah.

We sparred for a few minutes, and the big boys got impatient and shouted for action. So, at last, I forced myself to aim straight at his face and hit him hard in one eye. I was ashamed at once and sorry for him because I knew what it was like to be punched. But, although he was half-hearted about it and didn't fly into a killing rage, he went on fighting, and I hit him in the face again. The big boys cheered me and patted me on the shoulder. I felt flushed with victory, but I hated them too. They disgusted me, for they were risking nothing themselves and nobody was punching their faces. I hated myself a bit for playing up to them. I was hoping Hannah would run away, and I wouldn't chase him very fast, but he suddenly kicked me.

Dirty foul! One of the spectators was so hot on fair play that he was making to kick Hannah from behind to prove it, but he missed him. I was smarting slightly from the kick on the shin and justifying myself when I hit him again. And then it got hellish. He was either blinded or posing as blind: It doesn't matter which, because he just stood with his hands in front of his face and I punched through his hands and hit him again and again. Finally, a man working in a garden across the street came over and stopped the fight. He told the big boys off and said I was a bully.

'He hit me first!' I said.

'Get away home out of here,' the man said, and I went.

Class discussion

How did the boy get involved in a fight which he did not want?
Why did the older boys want him to fight?

What were the boy's feelings during his fight with the boy called Hannah?

Why do crowds gather round when a fight starts?
Why do they watch the fight instead of trying to stop it?

Suggest what the boy was thinking on his way home after the fight.
Do you think he was feeling pleased with himself or ashamed?

In groups

- Talk about any fights you have had.
  How did you feel about the fight while it was happening and afterwards? How do you feel about it now?

- Choose someone from the group to act as secretary and work together to produce a statement giving the group's views about fighting. You must produce a statement of views that all the members of the group agree with.

- Each group's statement should then be read to the class, in turn, by the secretaries. When all the statements have been read, discuss any ways in which they are different.

- See if you can produce a statement about fighting that everyone in the class agrees with. Get your teacher to write it on the board.

FOR YOUR FOLDER

Copy the statement from the board into your folder, then, write a paragraph giving your own views. Call it 'My views on fighting'.

Bullying

Who gets picked on?

Pocket money

'I can't explain what happens to my cash.'
I can, but can't — not to my Mum and Dad.
'Give us ten pee or get another bash' —

That's where it goes. And though their questions crash
Like blows, and though they're getting mad,
I can't explain what happens to my cash;

How can I tell the truth? I just rehash
Old lies. The others have and I'm the had:
'Give us ten pee or get another bash.'

'For dinner Dad? . . . just sausages and mash.'
'That shouldn't make you broke by Wednesday, lad.'
I can't explain. What happens to my cash —

My friends all help themselves. I get the ash
Of fags I buy and give, get none. 'Too bad.
Give us ten pee or get another bash

For being You.' And still I feel the thrash
Of stronger, firmer hands than mine. The sad
Disgust of living like a piece of trash.
I can't explain what happens to my cash.
'Give us ten pee or get another bash.'

Mick Gowar

In pairs

1   Imagine that the boy in the poem is your friend. He has told you what is happening and wants you to promise not to tell anybody else about it. What would you do?
a)   Promise not to tell anyone and leave it at that.
b)   Try to persuade him to tell his parents.
c)   Try to persuade him to tell a teacher.
d)   Tell him to stand up to the boys who are bullying him.
e)   Tell a teacher about it yourself.
f)   Any other suggestions?
2   What sort of people bully others?
Is there such a thing as a typical bully?
3   Bullying can be mental as well as physical.
List some examples of mental bullying.
4   Are certain types of people more likely to get bullied than others? Why?

Study this list. Pick out the people you think are more likely to get bullied:
a)   someone who is very clever;
b)   someone who is always telling tales;
c)   someone who is good at games;
d)   someone who is no good at games;
e)   someone who cries easily;
f)   someone who can stand up for herself or himself;
g)   someone who is a loner;
h)   someone who has a lot of friends;
i)   someone who is bossy;
j)   someone who thinks they know everything;
k)   someone who will not share;
l)   someone who enjoys a laugh;
m)   someone who doesn't like getting dirty;
n)   someone who flies into a temper easily;
o)   someone whose parents are very rich;
p)   someone who is bigheaded.
Can you think of any other people who are likely to get bullied, who are not included in this list?
5   Now, look through the list again. Think about the people you said were less likely to get bullied. Suggest situations in which they might be bullied.

Frankie's problem

Frankie goes to your school. She is your friend, but she is in another class. She does not come to school one day, so you assume she must be ill. At dinner time you go round to her house to see how she is. You find her sitting in the living room watching tv. She seems all right, but when you ask her how she is, she bursts into tears. She tells you that another girl in her class is making her life a misery — calling her names, making snide remarks, hiding her things and hitting her. She is so upset that she has stayed away from school. It'll be all right, she says, because her mum will write her a note.

Can you help Frankie? Decide what advice you would give her.

Class discussion

Discuss in class your answers to all the questions you worked on in pairs.

24

Name-calling and nicknames

Class discussion

Look carefully at the photograph. Do you think some of these children have nicknames? What might they be?

Which of the children do you think is most likely to be teased? Why?

In pairs

'Sticks and stones may break my bones, but words can never hurt me.' Do you agree, or is name-calling hurtful?

What is the difference between name-calling and using nicknames? Do you think nicknames are harmless or can they be hurtful?

What is the difference between teasing and bullying? List some examples of behaviour which you regard as teasing and some examples of behaviour which you regard as bullying. Then, compare your list with those of other groups.

In groups

Role play
Work in groups of four. Plan and act out a series of scenes in which three of you gang up on a fourth person and tease him or her. Take it in turns to be the person being teased. After you have acted out several scenes, talk about what it feels like to be the person who is being teased. Before you begin, make a list of reasons why a person may get teased, e.g. they wear glasses, come bottom in a test, burst into tears when told off etc.

Work in groups of four or five. Act out a series of scenes in which a person is bullied by a group of other children who threaten to beat her or him up. EITHER work out your own scenes, OR develop scenes around these phrases:
'Do as we say or else . . .'
'If you split on us, you'll be sorry . . .'
'If you do that again, we'll . . .'
'Give us 10p each or . . .'

Why Poke Fun?

Picking on those who are different

One reason why some children get picked on is because they are different in some way. Kizzy Lovell is different because she is half-gypsy, a diddakoi, and she lives in a gypsy wagon. So the other children in the class call her names and poke fun at her appearance and behaviour, which they find strange.

Group discussion

How do the other children treat Kizzy?
How does Kizzy feel?
Why do the class ignore Mrs Blount's warning and break their promises to her?
Could Mrs Blount have said anything else to the class that might have made them alter their behaviour towards Kizzy?

Diddakoi.
Tinker.
Tinkety-tink.
Gypsy, gypsy joker, get a red hot poker.
Rags an' tags.
Clothes pegs. Who'll buy my clothes-pegs?
  — only they said 'cloes-pegs'.
Who'll buy my flowers? — only they said 'flahrs'.
Diddakoi.

'If anyone,' said the teacher, Mrs Blount, in the classroom, 'any*one*,' and her eyes looked sternly along the lines of tables filled with boys and girls, 'teases or bullies or jeers at Kizzy Lovell, they will answer for it to me.'

Twenty-eight pairs of eyes looked back at Mrs Blount blandly and innocently: 'As if we would,' they seemed to say. The twenty-ninth pair, Kizzy's, looked down at her table; she had a curious burning in her ears.

'To me,' said Mrs Blount. 'We shall not have such behaviour in this school.' But they would; silent and small, Kizzy knew that.

'Kizzy must be short for something,' Mrs Blount had asked her, 'What is your real name, dear?'

'Kizzy.'

Mrs Blount had touched a sore spot; in Kizzy's family, as in some gypsy clans, a child is given three names: a secret one whispered by its mother the moment it is born and, when it is grown, whispered again into the child's ear; a private or 'wagon' name which is used only by its own people, and a third open name by which it is known to the world. Kizzy seemed only to have one, but that was because she was what they called her, a 'diddakoi', not all gypsy. 'We don't say gypsies now. We say travellers,' Mrs Blount told the children. Kizzy's father, pure Rom, had married an Irish girl, but Kizzy looked gypsy to the children and they were half fascinated, half repelled by her brownness and the little gold rings in her ears — none of the other

girls had golden earrings. There was one boy Kizzy liked, big Clem Oliver, 'I thought gypsies had black eyes,' said Clem Oliver. 'Yours are dark, dark brown. They're nice — and these are pretty.' He touched the gold rings and Kizzy glowed and, 'My Gran has gold sov'reigns for her earrings,' she told Clem.

'Never seen sov'reigns,' said Clem in awe. Clem made Kizzy feel bigger, not small and frightened, big an' warm, thought Kizzy. Clem, though, was in an older class; she only saw him at break times, and the others teased. 'More than teased,' said Mrs Blount.

'But, Mildred, if you forbid people to do something, doesn't it usually make them want to do it even more?' asked Miss Olivia Brooke. Mrs Blount and her husband were lodging with Miss Brooke in the village until their own new house was built and she had told her about Kizzy. 'Doesn't it?' asked Miss Brooke.

'Well, what would you have done?'

'Could you, perhaps, have interested them in the little girl? Made her romantic. Gypsies . . .'

'Travellers,' corrected Mrs Blount.

'I like the old name. Gypsies have a romantic side. If, perhaps, you had told them stories . . .' but Mrs Blount said she preferred to use her own methods and, 'I want you to give me your promise,' she told the class, 'that there will be no more teasing of Kizzy,' and she even asked them, child by child, 'Do you promise?'

'Mary Jo, do you promise?'

'Yes, Mrs Blount.'

'Prudence Cuthbert, do you?'

'Yes, Mrs Blount,' said Prue.

'Yes, Mrs Blount . . . Yes, Mrs Blount,' the answers came back, glib and meek — what Mrs Blount did not know was that every girl said it with her fingers crossed. Kizzy saw that from her seat at the back of the room and knew, as soon as Mrs Blount was out of the way, it would start again. *Tinker . . . diddakoi . . . gypsy . . . clothes pegs . . . old clothes . . .*

Kizzy had come to school in new clothes, or thought she had. Traveller women seldom buy new clothes from shops; they make them or beg them or buy them at country jumble sales, but hers had looked to Kizzy brand new; she loved the tartan skirt and red jersey, the school blue blazer all of them wore, white socks, but, 'Wearing Prue Cuthbert's clothes,' the girls jeered.

'They're mine,' said Kizzy.

'Now. They were Prue's. Prue's mum gave them for you.' Prudence Cuthbert was the worst of the girls and that night Kizzy had put the clothes down a hollow in one of the old apple trees full of dead leaves and water. Her grandmother had lammed her but Kizzy did not care; no one could wear them after that, and next day she wore her own clothes for school. It had never occurred to her, or her Gran, that they were peculiar clothes, but they looked most peculiar in class: a limp strawberry-pink cotton dress too long for her — her vest showed at the top — a brown cardigan that had been a boy's larger than Kizzy, but if she pushed the sleeves up it was not much too big; some of the buttons had come off but Gran had found two large safety-pins.

How much do you really know about gypsies?

Children who are different are sometimes treated badly because the other children are *prejudiced* against them. A person who is prejudiced is someone who forms an opinion that is not based on facts. People are often prejudiced against gypsies — or travellers as they prefer to be called — simply because they live a different way of life, living in caravans rather than houses. There are about 35 000–40 000 travellers in England and approximately 8000 caravans.

> I tell you, I wouldn't go into a house. I've been bred and born to this life and I'd rather die this way. I have a daughter who had to go into a house, but it's driving her up the wall. I don't think she'll stick it, because she's not used to it, she's been born to a different life. It's like asking you to live in a caravan. If I had to go into a house I'd die. I'd miss the air; I wouldn't be able to breathe.

In pairs

> People who live in houses often go for their holidays in caravans, but they look down on people who live in caravans all the year round. It doesn't make sense.

Discuss this view. Why shouldn't people live in caravans on sites rather than in houses or flats, if they prefer to do so?

> We should respect travelling families and their customs, rather than pick on travellers just because they are different

What do you really know about travellers and their customs? Make a list of the questions you would like to ask a traveller about her/his way of life, if you could interview one. Then, use the library to find out the true facts about travellers and write the answers to your questions in your folder.

A Matter of Custom

In Britain

In groups

Each culture has its own customs. Traditional British customs include . . .

. . . having pancakes on Shrove Tuesday

. . . setting off fireworks on November 5th to celebrate Guy Fawkes' night

Traditionally, the main British family celebration is Christmas. Today, Britain is a multi-cultural society, so the main celebration varies from family to family. Whatever the main celebration is, each family often has its own special customs. Here is one family's own special Christmas ritual:

'In our family we open presents immediately after breakfast. They are all arranged on chairs in the sitting-room, one chair for each person and we all charge in armed with knives and scissors and fall upon them like vultures or starving wolves. Rory tears his open without a glance at the label and so fast it needs both parents to make a list of who has sent him what.'

In pairs

Talk about the main celebration in your families and about any special rituals your families have.

In Lesotho

Lesotho is an African country, completely surrounded by South Africa. Its name means mountain kingdom, which is very apt, as it is the only country in the world where all the land is over 1000 metres above sea level. Its people, the Basotho, still keep many of the traditional customs handed down to them over the centuries.

When grandmother died we had a big feast; when my younger sister, Mampe, was born, we didn't have a feast at all. We honour our dead people and show them respect by having a celebration; when a baby is born we don't want to let the spirits know in case they bring harm.

Grandmother was the person who organised the feasts to show respect to the ancestors, and prayed to them about problems. Even father used to consult her when he was worried. When she died the men dug the grave while the women prepared the food. Relations came from everywhere, even Maseru, on the buses and taxis, walking from the main gravel road to the village. Many men came on horses. We have only two cars in the village, the Chief's and the shopkeeper's, so most people had to walk. People came to look at the body and then she was carried in a coffin to the grave. In order of kinship the men covered the coffin with handfuls of earth. The women are not allowed too close. We sang some hymns and returned home where everyone had to wash their hands in a special bowl of water. Then we feasted on bread, meat and *joala*.*

Mampe was born at home. As soon as mother felt the baby coming she called her mother and some older women who boiled herbs for mother to drink to help the labour. When the baby was born, some dried herbs were burnt and mother and the baby were held in the smoke to keep the evil spirits away. Then one old lady took a bucket of water, ran to find my father and poured it over him! By that he knew that a girl was born; if it had been a boy, she would have beaten him with a stick.

For three months, mother and Mampe had to remain inside the house, and no man was allowed to visit. Two reeds were pushed in to the thatch near the door to tell everyone that there was a new baby inside. If she came out, she had to cover her head and not look up or she might cause a hail storm. The first time it rained, Mampe was put outside naked to get wet, which prevents her from becoming a thief. Mampe means 'mother of ugliness'. She is a very pretty baby but we call her ugly to deceive the bad spirits.

* local beer

Class discussion

Are there any customs that are usually observed in your culture when a person dies or a person is born? Talk about different funeral and birth customs which you have either read or heard about.

Superstitions

Every culture has its own superstitions. Here are some more from Lesotho:
- Spilling water brings lightning.
- A black cat brings bad luck.
- Never borrow salt after dark.
- If you kick a stone with the left foot, bad luck comes.
- Girls should never walk through a herd of animals, as it breaks the medicine that protects them from harm.
- If you see a green fly, it is bad luck.

FOR YOUR FOLDER

In pairs, do a project about superstitions. Talk to adults and see if they can tell you any interesting superstitions, and use the library to find out about superstitions in other cultures. You may find it helpful to organise your project into separate sections under different headings such as: numbers and dates; horseshoes, ladders and other objects; animals and birds; trees, flowers and fruits.

Here is an extract about sneezing:

'In Flanders, people used to think that if you sneezed when you were talking or making a bargain it proved you were telling the truth. The Chinese believe that a sneeze on New Year's Day means you'll have bad luck in the coming year. The Japanese believe that if you sneeze once, it is because someone is praising you. If you sneeze twice you are being blamed for something. If you sneeze three times, it just means you are ill!'

Let's Celebrate

Hindu festivals

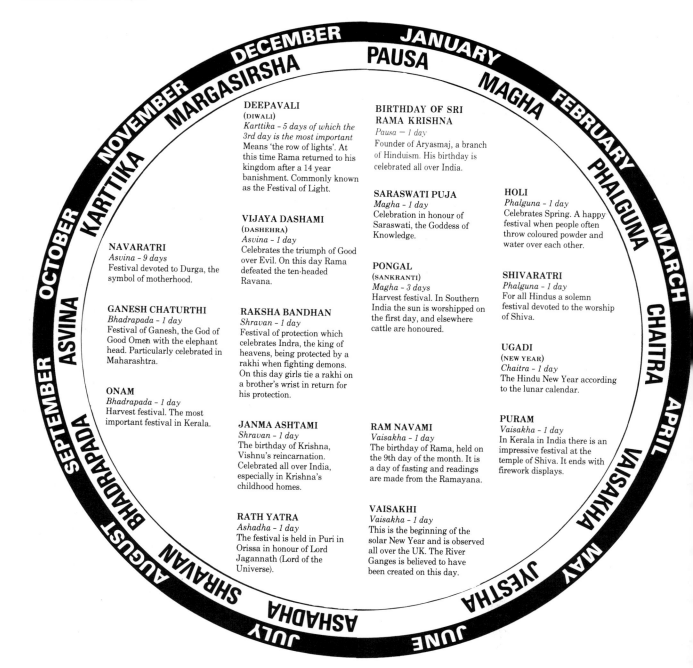

DEEPAVALI
(DIWALI)
Karttika – 5 days of which the 3rd day is the most important
Means 'the row of lights'. At this time Rama returned to his kingdom after a 14 year banishment. Commonly known as the Festival of Light.

VIJAYA DASHAMI
(DASHEHRA)
Asvina – 1 day
Celebrates the triumph of Good over Evil. On this day Rama defeated the ten-headed Ravana.

RAKSHA BANDHAN
Shravan – 1 day
Festival of protection which celebrates Indra, the king of heavens, being protected by a rakhi when fighting demons. On this day girls tie a rakhi on a brother's wrist in return for his protection.

JANMA ASHTAMI
Shravan – 1 day
The birthday of Krishna, Vishnu's reincarnation. Celebrated all over India, especially in Krishna's childhood homes.

RATH YATRA
Ashadha – 1 day
The festival is held in Puri in Orissa in honour of Lord Jagannath (Lord of the Universe).

NAVARATRI
Asvina – 9 days
Festival devoted to Durga, the symbol of motherhood.

GANESH CHATURTHI
Bhadrapada – 1 day
Festival of Ganesh, the God of Good Omen with the elephant head. Particularly celebrated in Maharashtra.

ONAM
Bhadrapada – 1 day
Harvest festival. The most important festival in Kerala.

BIRTHDAY OF SRI RAMA KRISHNA
Pausa — 1 day
Founder of Aryasmaj, a branch of Hinduism. His birthday is celebrated all over India.

SARASWATI PUJA
Magha – 1 day
Celebration in honour of Saraswati, the Goddess of Knowledge.

PONGAL
(SANKRANTI)
Magha – 3 days
Harvest festival. In Southern India the sun is worshipped on the first day, and elsewhere cattle are honoured.

RAM NAVAMI
Vaisakha – 1 day
The birthday of Rama, held on the 9th day of the month. It is a day of fasting and readings are made from the Ramayana.

VAISAKHI
Vaisakha – 1 day
This is the beginning of the solar New Year and is observed all over the UK. The River Ganges is believed to have been created on this day.

HOLI
Phalguna – 1 day
Celebrates Spring. A happy festival when people often throw coloured powder and water over each other.

SHIVARATRI
Phalguna – 1 day
For all Hindus a solemn festival devoted to the worship of Shiva.

UGADI
(NEW YEAR)
Chaitra – 1 day
The Hindu New Year according to the lunar calendar.

PURAM
Vaisakha – 1 day
In Kerala in India there is an impressive festival at the temple of Shiva. It ends with firework displays.

Hindus use the lunar calendar which means that the months start with each new moon. The first month of the year is Vaisakha and New Year's day is in the first or second week of April.

FOR YOUR FOLDER

The chart shows the main festivals of the Hindu year.
In pairs, draw a similar chart showing the main festivals of another year, e.g. the Christian, the Jewish, the Muslim, or the Sikh year.

ew Year festivities

The Chinese New Year

he Chinese New Year occurs during January or ebruary and is called Yuan Tan. Families and iends exchange gifts and there are spectacular reet processions.

The street processions always include a huge aper dragon, which represents strength and od luck. The dragon is made from pieces of amboo covered with either paper or cloth. Some the dragons are so big that it takes fifty people hold them together, as they dance through the reets.

The Chinese believe that evil spirits are about New Year. So firecrackers are set off to drive em away. Some families put strips of red paper und the doors and windows to keep the spirits it. Red paper is used because red is regarded as lucky colour.

The Jewish New Year

he Jewish New Year is called Rosh Hashanah nd occurs around September/October. It is the liest time of the year for the Jews and they tend services in the synagogue. During the rvice a ram's horn, called a shofar, is blown. he Bible says that Moses used a shofar to mmon his people to hear the Ten ommandments.

At the New Year, each Jew thinks about how e or she has behaved during the past year and akes resolutions for the future.

Hogmanay

In Scotland, New Year's Eve is called Hogmanay. In some towns and villages, an old boat or a straw figure called 'The Auld Wife' used to be burned or a blazing tar barrel was rolled through the streets. This represented the burning up of the remains of the old year.

Many Scottish families nowadays celebrate with a party, and the custom of 'first footing' is still widely observed. It used to be thought that the first person to enter your house on New Year's Day would influence whether you had good or bad luck during the coming year. A dark-haired man is supposed to bring good luck, especially if he is carrying a piece of coal. In the past, when the first-footer arrived, no one had to speak until he had put the coal on the fire.

The Muslim New Year

The Muslims use a calendar based on the moon rather than the sun. So the Muslim year is eleven days shorter than the calendar years which are calculated by the sun. This means that the New Year comes at a different time each year. The Muslim New Year's day is the first day of the month of Muharram. It is a holy day on which the Muslims read their holy book, the Koran, and tell stories of the Prophet Muhammad.

Planning a Project

Learning how to learn

This unit gives you a chance to work as a member of a group on a research project. The aim is not only to help you find out more about a topic that interests you, but also to help you learn some of the skills of *how* to learn. These are skills such as:
- decision-making
- organising and planning
- discussing and negotiating
- framing questions and seeking information
- meeting deadlines
- reporting both orally and in writing.

These are the sorts of skills that will help you a you move up the school and later on in life, bot at work and in your social life.

In order to help you to think about what you are doing and what you are learning, you are asked to keep a record of your activities in a project diary. Suggestions on how to keep your diary are given on the next page.

Doing your project — a step-by-step guide

Here are some of the steps or processes that you will have to go through when doing your research project:

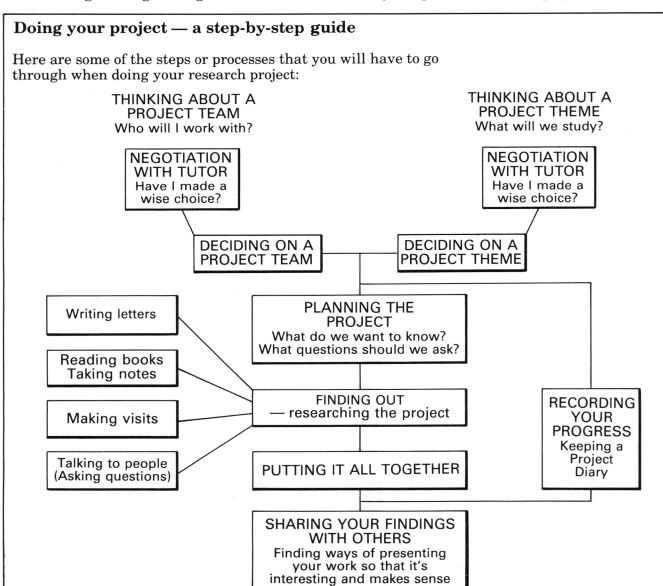

THINKING ABOUT A
PROJECT TEAM
Who will I work with?

THINKING ABOUT A
PROJECT THEME
What will we study?

NEGOTIATION
WITH TUTOR
Have I made a
wise choice?

NEGOTIATION
WITH TUTOR
Have I made a
wise choice?

DECIDING ON A
PROJECT TEAM

DECIDING ON A
PROJECT THEME

Writing letters

Reading books
Taking notes

Making visits

Talking to people
(Asking questions)

PLANNING THE
PROJECT
What do we want to know?
What questions should we ask?

FINDING OUT
— researching the project

PUTTING IT ALL TOGETHER

RECORDING
YOUR
PROGRESS
Keeping a
Project
Diary

SHARING YOUR FINDINGS
WITH OTHERS
Finding ways of presenting
your work so that it's
interesting and makes sense

Keeping a project diary

When you do a project, you are taking a lot of responsibility for yourself. In a way you are taking on part of the job of the teacher, because you and the other members of your group are educating *yourselves* about the subject you have decided to study. Your teacher may help you and give you advice about the best way of going about things, but *you* are in the driving seat.

It is very important, therefore, that you learn to drive well. You will almost certainly make mistakes, but as long as you learn from those mistakes, then your time will not have been wasted. The best way to learn from both your successes and your failures is to keep a careful record of everything you do in a project diary.

In groups

How to fill in your project diary

Keep your project diary on file paper which you can put in your folder.

Fill in your diary after each session that you work on your project. Allow some time at the end of each session for filling in your diary.

Keep a record of the date, the time you spent and the work you did. Write some comments on how you worked and what you learned. Write down your plans for the next session.

4   Before you fill in the work done and comments sections of your project diary, discuss with your group what each of you has done and how you have worked. Think about *how* you all work, both as a group and as individuals. Consider these questions:

Did you have a discussion at the start of the session to decide what to do?
Did you help each other out?
Did you make any group decisions?
Did you get on well together?
Did you have any arguments?
Was anyone bossy — and if so, how did the rest feel about this?
Did anyone let the group down by not doing her/his share of the work?

5   A successful project depends on good planning. Ask yourself what resources you will need for your next session, e.g. a tape-recorder, books or leaflets from the library. Do you need to copy up some notes or to write a letter before the next session? Do you need to ask permission to go on a visit? Always think ahead.

Above all, in your project diary, be honest. Record both your successes and your failures and say what *you* think. That's how you learn.

An entry from a project diary

DATE: 18th January 1986.

TIME SPENT: 3/4 hour.

WORK DONE: We looked up the names of vets and telephoned one called Ms Harper. She gave us an appointment for next Thursday. Then we worked out some questions to ask her, about how well people look after their dogs.

COMMENTS: I learned how to use the Yellow Pages to find out addresses and telephone numbers. We had an argument about the questions to ask. Mandy was bossy but we had some good ideas.

PLAN FOR NEXT SESSION: Finish working out questions. Ask permission to go to the vets.

Using the Library

How libraries are organised

When you want to find information on a topic for a project or homework, an obvious place to go is either the school or public library. You will find that most libraries are organised in a similar way, and so it is important to understand how books are arranged, so that you can always find the ones you want.

The three main sections

There are three main sections in most libraries:

The reference section
This contains books you are likely to want to refer to in order to find out a particular piece of information, rather than books you will want to read from cover to cover. It includes encyclopedias, dictionaries, atlases and maps, directories and gazeteers. Because such books are in constant use and are large and expensive you are not usually allowed to take them away from the library.

The fiction section
This consists of story books — novels and anthologies. The books in the fiction section are usually arranged in alphabetical order of the authors' surnames. Public libraries have junior fiction sections and adult fiction sections, and there may also be a teenage fiction section.

The non-fiction section
This contains all the books that are factual, information books rather than fictional story books. Such books range from true life adventure stories and books about famous people, to books about hobbies and textbooks on all kinds of subjects. The books in the non-fiction section are usually arranged by subjects rather than alphabetically by the authors' surnames. For example, all the history books are grouped on one set of shelves and all the sports books on another set of shelves.

How non-fiction books are classified

To help you find the non-fiction book you want, libraries use a system of numbers. Each book is given a number and details of the number are put on the book's spine. You can trace a book by finding out its number. Then, by looking at a plan of the library you can work out on which shelf to find it.

There are various systems of numbering books but the one most commonly used is called the **Dewey Decimal System**. Each book is put into one of ten main classes. These classes are numbered as follows:

The Dewey System of Classification	
000	GENERAL
100	PHILOSOPHY
200	RELIGION
300	SOCIAL SCIENCE
400	LANGUAGES
500	SCIENCE
600	APPLIED SCIENCE
700	FINE ARTS
800	LITERATURE
900	GEOGRAPHY/BIOGRAPHY/HISTORY

Within these main classes each particular subject is given its own number. For example, the Science class is divided into subjects as follows:

500	SCIENCE GENERAL
510	MATHEMATICS
520	ASTRONOMY
530	PHYSICS
540	CHEMISTRY
550	PHYSICAL GEOGRAPHY
560	PALAEONTOLOGY*
570	BIOLOGY
580	BOTANY
590	ZOOLOGY

* The study of fossils

Each class is given a number of shelves in the library. The shelf point, where the books in a particular class are stocked, varies from library to library depending on the layout.

Finding a book

The way to go about finding a book you want is to look it up in the library's catalogue to see if the library has a copy. Libraries keep lists called indexes of the books they stock. There are usually two indexes — an index of authors and an index of subjects and there may also be an index of titles. The flow chart on the opposite page shows you how to use the indexes.

How to find the book you want

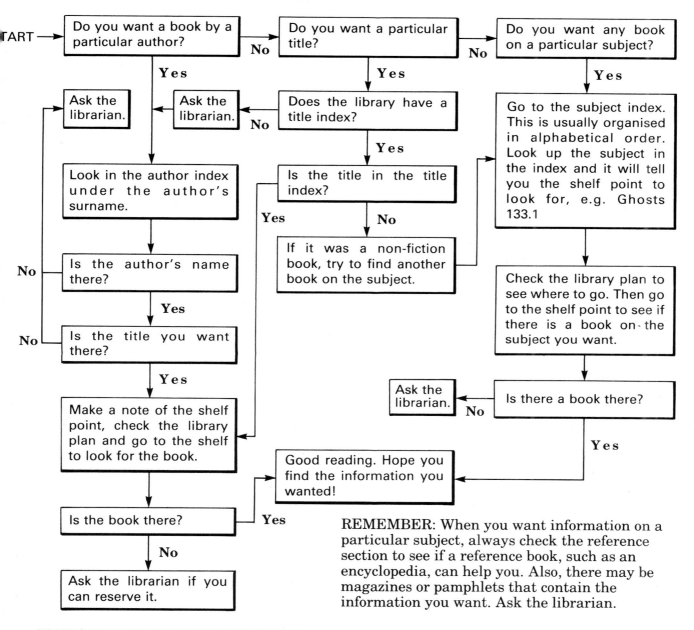

REMEMBER: When you want information on a particular subject, always check the reference section to see if a reference book, such as an encyclopedia, can help you. Also, there may be magazines or pamphlets that contain the information you want. Ask the librarian.

FOR YOUR FOLDER

Work with a partner and investigate your library.

1 Draw a plan of the library. Mark in the following: reference section, fiction section, non-fiction shelves (label where each of the ten main classes of books are shelved), the issue counter, the catalogue indexes etc.

2 List five topics that are in the news at present. In which section of the library would you find books on these topics? Write down the subject classification number for each topic. Use the flow chart to help you find a book on one of the topics.

Getting Information from Books

Use this flow chart to help you to find information from books for your research project.

Section 1

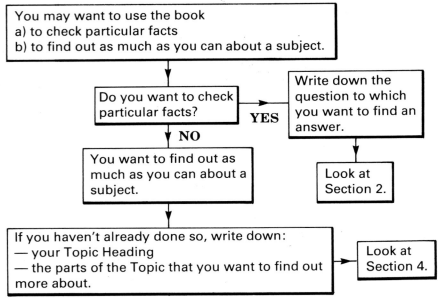

You may want to use the book
a) to check particular facts
b) to find out as much as you can about a subject.

Do you want to check particular facts? **YES** → Write down the question to which you want to find an answer. → Look at Section 2.

NO ↓

You want to find out as much as you can about a subject.

If you haven't already done so, write down:
— your Topic Heading
— the parts of the Topic that you want to find out more about. → Look at Section 4.

Section 2

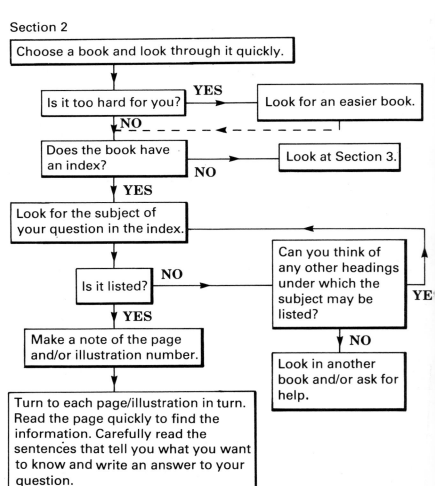

Choose a book and look through it quickly.

Is it too hard for you? **YES** → Look for an easier book.

NO

Does the book have an index? **NO** → Look at Section 3.

YES ↓

Look for the subject of your question in the index.

Is it listed? **NO** → Can you think of any other headings under which the subject may be listed? **YES**

NO ↓

Look in another book and/or ask for help.

YES ↓

Make a note of the page and/or illustration number.

Turn to each page/illustration in turn. Read the page quickly to find the information. Carefully read the sentences that tell you what you want to know and write an answer to your question.

Section 3

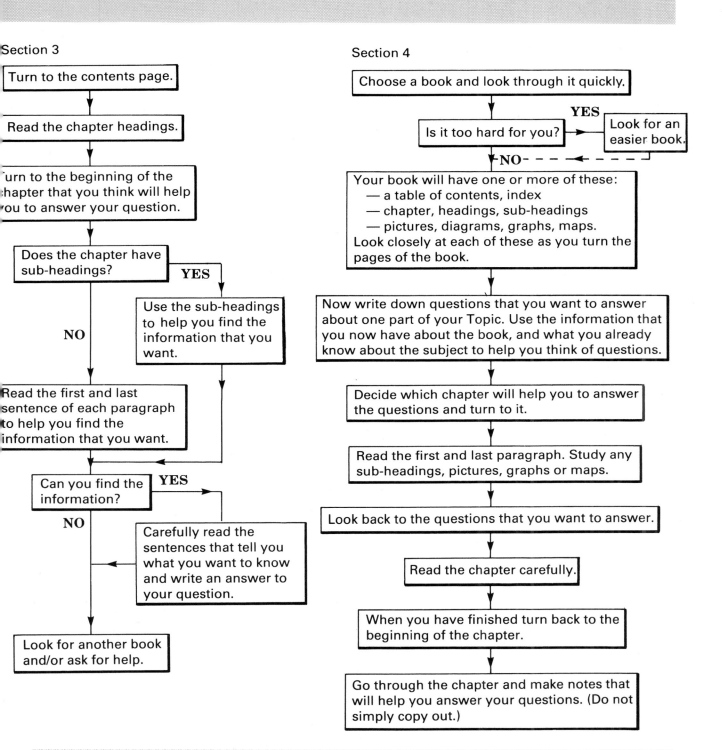

Turn to the contents page.

Read the chapter headings.

Turn to the beginning of the chapter that you think will help you to answer your question.

Does the chapter have sub-headings?

YES

Use the sub-headings to help you find the information that you want.

NO

Read the first and last sentence of each paragraph to help you find the information that you want.

Can you find the information?

YES

NO

Carefully read the sentences that tell you what you want to know and write an answer to your question.

Look for another book and/or ask for help.

Section 4

Choose a book and look through it quickly.

Is it too hard for you?

YES

Look for an easier book.

NO

Your book will have one or more of these:
— a table of contents, index
— chapter, headings, sub-headings
— pictures, diagrams, graphs, maps.
Look closely at each of these as you turn the pages of the book.

Now write down questions that you want to answer about one part of your Topic. Use the information that you now have about the book, and what you already know about the subject to help you think of questions.

Decide which chapter will help you to answer the questions and turn to it.

Read the first and last paragraph. Study any sub-headings, pictures, graphs or maps.

Look back to the questions that you want to answer.

Read the chapter carefully.

When you have finished turn back to the beginning of the chapter.

Go through the chapter and make notes that will help you answer your questions. (Do not simply copy out.)

FOR YOUR FOLDER

Think about how the chart helped you find one piece of information that you needed for your project. List the various steps by which you found that information. Then, draw a step-by-step flow chart showing the steps by which you found the book and the information you wanted.

How Do I Look?

Me

There are something like 4500 million people in the world. Some are tall, some are short. Some are fat, some are thin. Some have dark hair, some have fair hair. Some are dark-skinned, some are light-skinned.

Each person is unique, with his or her own physical features and characteristics. Here is a poem in which Jimi Rand writes about himself and his uniqueness:

A Black Man's Song

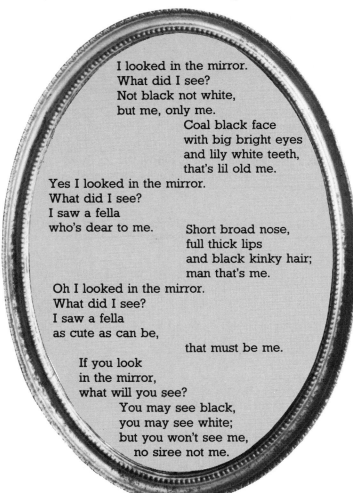

I looked in the mirror.
What did I see?
Not black not white,
but me, only me.
Coal black face
with big bright eyes
and lily white teeth,
that's lil old me.
Yes I looked in the mirror.
What did I see?
I saw a fella
who's dear to me.
Short broad nose,
full thick lips
and black kinky hair;
man that's me.
Oh I looked in the mirror.
What did I see?
I saw a fella
as cute as can be,
that must be me.
If you look
in the mirror,
what will you see?
You may see black,
you may see white;
but you won't see me,
no siree not me.

Jimi Rand

In pairs

If you were writing about your appearance, which of your features would you include in a description of yourself?
Choose someone to be your partner. Begin by working on your own and without talking to your partner, write a) a description of your appearance, and b) a description of your partner's appearance. Then, show each other what you have written. Whose description is the most accurate — your own or your partner's?

Passports

We use photographs and physical descriptions for purposes of identification on passports. A passport is a document issued to you by the country of which you are a citizen. You need a passport if you want to travel to another country and if you have not got a passport, you almost certainly won't be allowed to enter the other country.

2	DESCRIPTION *SIGNALEMENT*			
		Bearer Titulaire	Spouse Epouse	
Occupation Profession				
Place of birth Lieu de naissance				Bearer Titulaire
Date of birth Date de naissance				
Residence Résidence				
Height Taille		m	m	Spouse Epouse	Photo
Distinguishing marks Signes particuliers				

CHILDREN *ENFANTS*
Name Nom   Date of birth Date de naissance   Sex Sexe

Usual signature of bearer
Signature du titulaire

Usual signature of spouse
Signature de son épouse

The bearer (and spouse, if included) should sign opposite on rece...

FOR YOUR FOLDER

Study the page (above) from a British passport. Make a copy of the page and fill in the details that would appear on your passport.

Fingerprint facts

One feature which distinguishes you from everyone else is the pattern of your fingerprints. The pattern of each separate finger is different from the patterns of all the others. This is because the ridges on your fingertips vary in shape. So the ridge characteristics of each fingerprint are different. No two people have the same fingerprints and even the fingerprints of identical twins are different!

The patterns of your fingerprints do not change as you grow older, even though your skin becomes cracked and wrinkled with age. So your fingerprints can always be used to identify you.

Wherever you go, you tend to leave your fingerprints behind you. This is because the ridges of your fingertips are covered with tiny holes. These holes are the openings from which sweat escapes from the glands just beneath the surface of the skin. When you press your fingers on a smooth object, the small deposits of sweat join together and a print of the pattern is left on the object. You often cannot see the pattern clearly with the naked eye, so these prints are called latent prints. But if certain chemical powders are brushed over the prints they become visible. Photographs of the prints can be taken and they can be used to identify you.

Files of fingerprints can be kept on computers and a computer can identify you from your fingerprints in a matter of seconds. Who knows, in the future, we may use our fingerprints on documents instead of our signatures, as fingerprints are certainly harder to forge.

The pictures show the four main types of fingerprints.

Composite

Whorl

Arch

Loop

How to take your fingerprints

1 Coat a small piece of glass or metal with printer's ink.
2 Press the finger and thumb ridges against the inked surface.
3 Press the inked fingertips against a white card.

FOR YOUR FOLDER

EITHER take a set of your fingerprints, OR study your fingerprints under a magnifying glass. Write down what type of fingerprints you have.

Where Do You Come From?

Family histories

What make each of us different are the characteristics we have inherited from our parents and ancestors. Do you know which part of the world your family came from originally?

Although we all call ourselves British, not many of us actually had ancient Britons for our ancestors! Most of us probably had ancestors who came to Britain from other parts of the world.

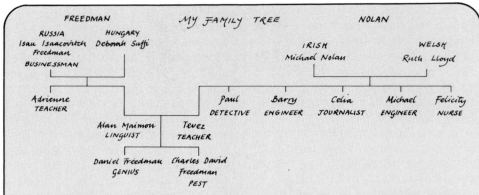

If my grandparents had met when they were young, they wouldn't have understood each other! They each came from some far corner of the earth, and came to Britain in an odd way.

My mother's mother was the daughter of a Welsh sailor, who was shipwrecked off Southport and never returned to Wales.

My mother's father was of Irish descent; his own father had come to England because of the potato famine. My grandfather was brought up near Liverpool, where my mother was born.

On my father's side, my grandmother was from a remote part of the Austro-Hungarian Empire. Her family settled in Manchester, but she now lives in Brighton.

My grandfather came from Russia and was called Isau Isaacovitch (that was only his first name). He was Jewish, and after the Revolution he felt persecuted, so he emigrated to America. The border guard who had to fill in the immigration form could not spell Isau Isaacovitch, so he filled in the form like this:

Name   Freedman, Charles David

Age   Unknown

Nationality   Russian

My grandpa was called Charlie from then on. When he moved to Britain he started a cloth business in George Street, Manchester. This is where my father was born.

When my mother was small, she lived in a very poor family. In contrast, my dad lived in a house with a chauffeur, maid and servants. During the war my dad escaped from numerous boarding schools, earning the name 'Houdini Freedman'.

My favourite relative is my Uncle Herbert, aged eighty, who is as thin as a rake and leaps around mending roofs. His spriteliness shows again in my grandma, whose exact age is dubious, but she has been telling us that she's seventy-nine for about a decade now.

Daniel Freedman

Who are your ancestors?

Here is what would happen to Prince Charles if he could go back to where he came from. What would happen to you?

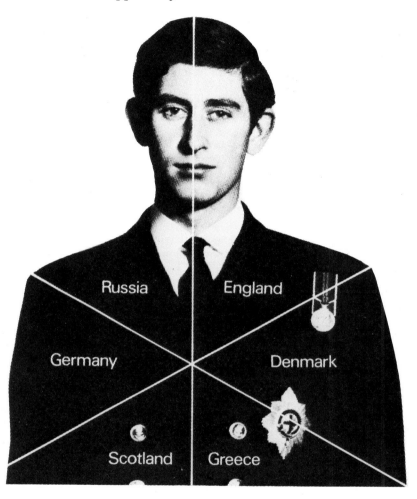

FOR YOUR FOLDER

1 EITHER talk to your parents and relatives about your own family history, OR talk to any adult you know who has an interesting family history. Make notes and then write about the family in the way that Daniel Freedman has written about his.
2 Draw a family tree for your family, or an imaginary family. As well as putting in people's occupations, put in the dates of their births and deaths (if known).
3 Do you have a favourite uncle or aunt, as Daniel Freedman does? Or one you particularly admire or remember because he or she is different from the others? Write a paragraph about your favourite uncle or aunt.

In groups

Use books in the reference and history sections of the library to find out when the Roman, Anglo-Saxon, Danish and Norman invasions of Britain took place. Then, find out about other groups of people who have come to live in Britain over the centuries, e.g. cloth-workers from the Netherlands in the 16th century, and in our own century, refugees from Russia and Eastern Europe, and Asians from Uganda, India, Pakistan and Bangladesh, and West Indians. Hang a large map of the world on the classroom wall and put tapes across it to show the various places from which people have come to Britain and the dates when they arrived.

What's in a Name?

Customs and origins

'I was named Helena by my mum. She got the name off the make-up she was using — Helena Rubenstein. I'm very glad she was not using anything like Rimmel.'   Helena

'My name is Lorenzo Lucas. I am very proud of my name because it is unique. My name is of Spanish origin and sometimes I feel that I am some kind of conquistador fighting and winning battles. I also like my name because it is all part of liking oneself and being happy to be alive. It also looks great on the back of a baseball jersey.'   Lorenzo

'I would have preferred to be called something like Salina or Charlene or Sarita because they aren't common names like mine. Most of my family have got common names like Jason, Ginny, Lloyd and Vincent.'   Alexandra

'I think I would have been a little happier with a macho name like Craig, Steve or something in that order. But I do suppose it could be worse.'   Kenneth, aged 16

'My name is Gavin. My dad told me it originated from the name Gawain. It has changed over the years. The name Gavin means white hawk. The name Gawain is a name that people sometimes had in the old days when knights were alive. There was a knight called Gawain. He had a white hawk on his shield.'   Gavin

Nowadays, most people have more than one name. The first people known to have had more than one name were the Chinese. The Emperor Fushi is said to have ordered the use of family names in about 2852 BC.

The Chinese usually have three names. The first name is a family name and comes from one of the 438 words in the Chinese sacred poem Po-Chia-Hsing. The second name is a generation name taken from a poem of between 20 and 30 characters adopted by each family. The third name is a milk name or personal name.

In western societies, many people have three names — two personal names, or given names, and a family name or surname. The given names consist of a first name and a middle name and are often called Christian names. The third name, or last name, is the surname. All three names together make up the person's legal name, as recorded on their birth certificate.

Other societies have their own traditions of naming. The name-system used by most Hindus in Britain is similar to the English name-system. There are one or more personal names, followed by the subcaste name (i.e. surname) which is used by the whole family.

Sikhs also usually have three names — a personal name which comes first, then a title name (SINGH for males and KAUR for females) and a subcaste name, borne by the whole family, e.g. Mohinder Singh Sandhu, Gurmit Kaur Sondh, Hardib Kaur Bassi. Often, however, the subcaste name is dropped, so that a person is called simply Mohinder Singh or Gurmit Kaur.

The Muslim naming-system is much more complex. A person may have two, three or four names — a personal name, one or two title names and a family name. But many people do not have family names and the personal name is often not the first one.

What do I mean?

All names have meanings, though most people today are unaware of what their personal names mean. For example, did you know that Barbara is a Greek name meaning stranger or that Douglas is a Celtic name meaning dark water?

The meaning of family names may be obvious if they have grown out of a person's surroundings (e.g. Hill), job (e.g. Carpenter), or the name of an ancestor (e.g. Johnson). But the meaning of many family names is not so clear.

The Origin and Meaning of Some Common Given Names

This table shows the origin and probable meaning of a number of given names. Many names are so old that scholars can only guess at their meaning.

Name	Origin	Meaning	Name	Origin	Meaning
Alexander	Greek	helper of humanity	Jeffrey	Teutonic	God's peace
Amy	French	beloved	Jennifer	Celtic	white wave
Andrew	Greek	manly	Joan	Hebrew	gift of God
Ann, Anne	Hebrew	grace	John	Hebrew	God's gracious gift
Anthony	Latin	praiseworthy or priceless	Joseph	Hebrew	the Lord shall add
Barbara	Greek	stranger	Judith, Judy	Hebrew	Jewess or praised
Benjamin	Hebrew	son of the right hand	Julia, Julie	Latin	downy face
Brian	Celtic	strong	Karen	Greek	pure
Carl, Charles	Teutonic	man	Laura	Latin	laurel
Catherine	Greek	pure	Louis	Greek	desirable
Christopher	Greek	Christ bearer	Margaret	Greek	pearl
Daniel	Hebrew	God is my judge	Mark	Latin	of Mars, the Roman god of war
Darlene	Anglo-Saxon	darling			
Deborah	Hebrew	bee	Mary	Hebrew	bitter
Dennis	Greek	of Dionysus, the Greek god of wine	Matthew	Hebrew	gift of God
			Melanie	Greek	black
Dorothy	Greek	gift of God	Michael	Hebrew	godlike
Douglas	Celtic	dark water	Nancy	Hebrew	grace
Edward	Teutonic	rich guardian	Natalie	Latin	Christmas child
Elaine, Ellen	Greek	light	Patricia	Latin	of noble birth
Elizabeth	Hebrew	oath of God	Paul	Latin	little
Emily	Latin	industrious	Philip	Greek	lover of horses
Eric	Teutonic	kingly	Rachel	Hebrew	ewe
Francis, Frank	Teutonic	free	Richard	Teutonic	rule, hard
Frederick	Teutonic	peaceful ruler	Robert	Teutonic	bright fame
George	Greek	farmer	Ronald	Teutonic	advice, power
Gerald	Teutonic	strong with a spear	Samuel	Hebrew	God has heard
Gloria	Latin	glorious	Sara, Sarah	Hebrew	princess
Harold	Teutonic	warrior	Steven, Stephen	Greek	crown or garland
Helen	Greek	light	Susan, Susannah	Hebrew	lily
Henry	Teutonic	ruler of the home	Teresa, Theresa	Greek	harvester
James	Hebrew	may God protect, or one who takes the place of another	Theodore	Greek	gift of God
			Thomas	Aramaic	twin
			Virginia	Latin	pertaining to spring
Jane, Janet	Hebrew	gift of God	Walter	Teutonic	powerful ruler
Jean	Hebrew	gift of God	William	Teutonic	will, helmet

In groups

Use the information on these pages to prepare a short radio item called 'What's in a name?' If you need to find out more information, use the reference section in the library (see page 34). Discuss how you are going to present the information and write a script. Then record it and play it to the rest of the class. When you have heard all the recordings, decide which group's recording was the most successful and why.

FOR YOUR FOLDER

How was your name first chosen? How were the names of the other members of your family – your brothers and sisters, your parents and relatives – chosen? Ask your parents and other adult relatives. Then write a short paragraph about how your name was chosen.

Personal Tastes

I like...

We have seen how each person is unique, in terms of physical appearance, fingerprints and name. Each person has his or her own character too and we all have particular likes and dislikes. This is what a class of children had to say when they were asked to list the things they liked and the things they loathed.

I LIKE . . .	I LOATHE . . .
MacDonald's, Steve Cram, and being with my family.	Carrots, Jackanory and The News. *Pramjit*
Riding my bike, playing on my computer and travel.	Having a headache, dark chocolate and visiting people I don't know. *Hitaindra*
Buying new things, writing letters and eating pizza.	Waking up in the morning, washing the dishes and spinach. *Daljit*
Indian, Chinese and English food, mantlepieces, ornaments and new things.	Greasy food, punks and waiting for buses. *Smeeta*
Collecting rubbers, leather coats and grandfather clocks.	Pictures of babies, freckles and nail varnish on toes. *Michelle*
Going swimming, long finger nails and fashion clothes.	Long-haired boys and going to the dentist. *Tina*
Looking from the window, flowers and teddy bears.	Being bored, being hurt and fighting. *Paresh*
Snooker, snow and cool drinks.	Rainy days, classical music and snooker players who smoke. *Wandeep*
The seaside, trainers and TV.	Bullies, cats when they scratch and bees because they sting. *Steven*
Adventure playgrounds, coconut and American films.	Snobs, bitten finger nails and Coronation Street. *Lorna*

I LIKE . . .	I LOATHE . . .
White bread, walking and Fridays.	Brown bread, mud and bubble gum. *Natasha*
Fried eggs, Smash and fighting.	Girls, fat people and wasps. *Samuel*
Looking at a cloudy sky, being slim and making friends.	Racists, game shows and being hungry. *Kiran*
The colour green, chips with sauce and body popping.	Cowboy films, walking in mud and braces on my teeth. *Nina*
Jewellery, Indian films and neat gardens with lots of flowers.	Smoking, striped ties and jumble sales. *Nidhi*
Fireworks, my sister's baby and my uncle's dog.	Blood sports, vivisection and being late for school. *Joanne*
Rabbits, Christmas and making people laugh.	Mushy peas, assemblies and smoking. *Brian*
Sailing, climbing trees, and long car rides.	Coming to school, catching colds and OAPs. *Kevin*
Science fiction books, cricket and pretty girls.	School uniform, quiz shows and the rain. *Sean*
Smart boys, holidays and getting money.	Dandruff, The News and having injections. *Donna*
Horror films, pie and mash and BMX bikes.	Burnt toast, tall people and trouble-makers. *James*

...loathe...

In pairs

Study the chart of likes and dislikes. Pick out one person you think you might make friends with because you share the same likes and dislikes and *one* person you think you would be unlikely to make friends with because you have different opinions. Is your choice the same as your partner's?

Draw two columns on a sheet of paper and add the headings 'I like . . .' and 'I loathe . . .' Make a list of six things you like and six things you dislike. When you have finished, go through the list and put a number against each item showing the order in which you like and dislike the things you have listed — the thing you like best would have a 1 alongside it. Are your lists at all like your partners?

Tell your partner what it is that you particularly like and loathe about the things you have put on your lists.

Class discussion

Produce a large chart similar to the one in this book, giving details of the main likes and dislikes of the people in your class. Discuss the similarities and differences between the things you have listed.

If you asked a class of, a) 7-year-olds, and b) 16-year-olds to do the same exercise, in what ways do you think their lists would differ from yours?

If you asked your parents to make lists like this, what do you think they would put on their lists?

FOR YOUR FOLDER

If you had to fill in a personal profile, what would you put? Make your own 'Peculiarities and Preferences' profile and put it in your folder.

Personal profile

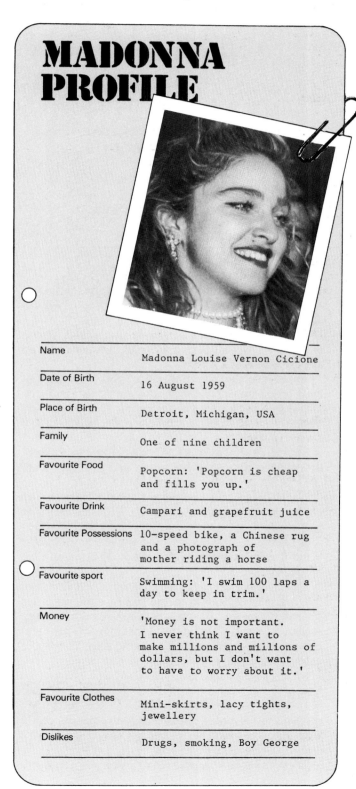

MADONNA PROFILE

Name	Madonna Louise Vernon Cicione
Date of Birth	16 August 1959
Place of Birth	Detroit, Michigan, USA
Family	One of nine children
Favourite Food	Popcorn: 'Popcorn is cheap and fills you up.'
Favourite Drink	Campari and grapefruit juice
Favourite Possessions	10-speed bike, a Chinese rug and a photograph of mother riding a horse
Favourite sport	Swimming: 'I swim 100 laps a day to keep in trim.'
Money	'Money is not important. I never think I want to make millions and millions of dollars, but I don't want to have to worry about it.'
Favourite Clothes	Mini-skirts, lacy tights, jewellery
Dislikes	Drugs, smoking, Boy George

Computers and You

At home in the future

What do you think the world will be like at the end of this century?

Group discussion

Talk about Tamara's and Tommy's home. Do you think that in the future you will live in a house like theirs?
What will homes be like in the future?
Will everybody live in computerised houses or only a few rich people?
2   Already computers play a large part in the lives of people who live in the developed countries of the world.
Make a group list of the ways in which computers play a part in the life of your families a) at home, b) at school, c) in shops, offices and a work, and d) in your leisure-time activities.

The computerised home

Tamara wakes to the sound of pop music. 'Hello, it's eight o'clock on Monday the twenty-third of February 1999. Please get up now. Thank you.'

Tamara's bedside alarm controller could switch on the light, open the curtains and turn the radio on to play pop music.

Sometimes the music was too loud, and Tamara had been up late on Sunday night putting the finishing touches to the program which she had written to make the alarm controller work under voice control.

'Shut up,' she said. Obediently, the music went down. The curtains drew again and the light went off.

According to the program it should have woken her up again in ten minutes time. Unfortunately she had made a mistake in the program and it didn't wake her again. Tamara would be late for school.

But Tommy's alarm watch went off normally, so he got up.

Meanwhile Dad, who was having breakfast, got the morning report from the home computer. 'It's snowing outside. The temperature is one degree below freezing. The central heating system and burglar alarm systems are working fine. There is a voicegram waiting. Thank you,' it said.

Mum played back the voicegram which was from a new client, telling her that he still wanted to meet her, if she could get to his office in the snow. She pressed the remote control button to start the car. It would need to warm up before she could take it out.

They collected the morning delivery at the door.

Milk, mail, the newspaper and the shopping they had ordered from the supermarket the night before on Teletex. (They were friendly with the delivery man who was a computer program author during the day.)

Dad woke Tamara up, and walked off through the snow to the local office building where he worked as an accountant for a large business. He'd play a game of squash with a friend on the office squash court before he started work. Tommy went out with him to catch the school bus.

Mum dialled up the road condition report on Teletex, flicking past the advertisements by the oil company which sponsored the report. The report told her that one road was blocked by the snow, but also told her how to get round the blockage. She tried to call her client, but his phone was busy, so she left a voicegram saying that she was coming. Then she bundled her work computer in its attaché case into the car and set off for her meeting.

She was a technical developments researcher for a number of small companies. She searched technical databases in New York, Tokyo and London for technical developments that her clients might want to know about and then sent the reports to her clients.

By the time she had eaten breakfast, Tamara had missed the school bus, so she had to dial the local taxi-bus to come and pick her up. Because she was late she would miss the computer spelling game at school. 'Never mind,' she thought. 'I'll be able to do it at home tonight.'

Class discussion

Compare your lists. Ask your teacher to draw a diagram on the board by writing the word COMPUTERS at the centre of the board and putting arrows from it to indicate the part computers play in different areas of your life. Copy this into your folder.

What recent developments in information technology have you read about or heard about from programmes such as *Tomorrow's World*?

Discuss the main changes that you think computers will bring about in your lives during the next ten years.

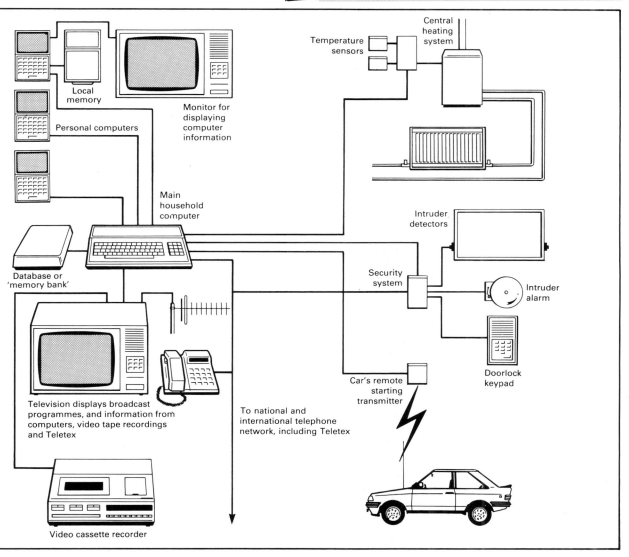

Local memory

Personal computers

Monitor for displaying computer information

Main household computer

Database or 'memory bank'

Television displays broadcast programmes, and information from computers, video tape recordings and Teletex

Video cassette recorder

To national and international telephone network, including Teletex

Temperature sensors

Central heating system

Intruder detectors

Security system

Intruder alarm

Doorlock keypad

Car's remote starting transmitter

Technology—Today and Tomorrow

Helping the handicapped

In the past, people who were handicapped were often cut off from the world, because they found it difficult to communicate. For many of them, new technology is revolutionising their lives. For example, devices have been developed to enable deaf people to use the telephone, blind people to write fluently and easily, and paralysed people to open and close doors. The pictures on this page show some of the ways that technology has begun to change the lives of the disabled.

Taking a few steps with the help of a computer. The micro-technology is on a belt strapped around the waist and this gives a series of stimulations to the leg muscles. This equipment is still experimental, but is already helping people who have been confined to a wheelchair for many years.

A mouth pointer is used to operate a keyboard.

A wide range of software has been developed for the blind and partially sighted. Luke uses an overlay keyboard to draw.

An expanded keyboard is being used here. These keyboard are useful for people who find finger control difficult.

twenty-five years' time

In 1975, the British National Committee for Cultural Cooperation in Europe organised a competition called Europe 2000. Young people were asked to write about what they thought life would be like in twenty-five years' time. Here are extracts from the winning entries written by 10- to 12-year-olds:

HOME LIFE
Bridget Atherton

In a quite up-to-date house the dining table is under the floor and when it is needed someone pulls a switch and the table comes up immediately. All the equipment in the kitchen is built in either the wall or on the counter tops.

All the waste except for paper and metal is put into a little machine which melts it and then it goes down a pipe into the sewage system.

Some people, only very rich people, have a kind of robot in their homes. It isn't a kind of robot with arms and legs, in fact it doesn't even do what you say. You have to press a button. The robot type things are used for different things, for instance you can buy one for doing the house work. You press a button and it vacuums the house.

When you go to the doctor because you feel there is something wrong with you he puts you in a machine which tests you to see what is wrong with you. I think the world in the year 2000 will be a nice place to live in.

FOOD AND WILDLIFE
Laura Whitehead

Meat and fish are scarce and very expensive in shops and restaurants. A lot of food is made from soya beans and other substitutes. Bread is also expensive even if you make your own. This is because a lot of food is imported from other countries by boat.

There are quite a few zoos in the cities as more animals are being killed in the wild, so most cities have about two zoos and safari parks nearby in the outskirts. In this way anyone can visit the zoos and take an interest in the preservation of wild animals. Anyone who brings their dog into the city leaves their dog in special kennels at the zoo.

THE ENVIRONMENT
Robert Ness

People will live in houses made of material such as plastic. They will be joined together in an interlocking pattern, making them easy to erect, dismantle and remove to a different site. All the segments will be fixed to a core which will house water, electricity and other services. The core will be almost self-sufficient, being able to produce heat from solar rays and pure water from rain water. The areas designated for community living will have open spaces with playing and recreational areas and landscape to provide a healthy and pleasant environment. The upkeep of the areas will be of a high standard and vandalism will be punished with severity.

The outer limits of the cities can be made into nature parks, etc, with fishing, boating and wildlife conservation areas. Providing we plan and properly preserve our cities of 2000 they can be places of beauty and enjoyment, otherwise we shall be living in a worse environment than the Victorians lived in.

FOR YOUR FOLDER

What do *you* think life will be like twenty-five years from now? Think carefully about how things might have changed. Jot down your ideas under headings such as: family life, work and play, clothes and fashions, building designs, transport, communications, the environment and education. Then, write a passage expressing your ideas about the world in twenty-five years' time. Before you begin, plan your writing by producing a flow chart to show the order in which you are going to present your ideas. Then, try to think of a way of beginning that will immediately catch your reader's attention.

Brush Up on Your Teeth

How much do you know?

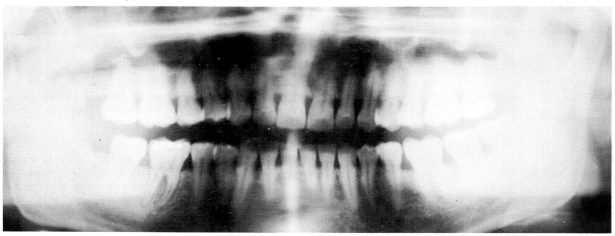

X-ray showing healthy teeth

Q. What is a tooth made of?
A. Most of the tooth is made of dentine, but your teeth have to be tough in order to be able to bite and chew hard foods. So, the outside of each tooth is covered with a hard layer of enamel. The tooth is supported by the gum and held firmly in place in your jawbone by long roots.

Q. What gives you toothache?
A. Usually it is because you have got tooth decay. Each tooth is alive and has its own supply of blood and nerves in the soft pulp at the centre of the tooth. If you have tooth decay, the nerves cause you to feel the pain which we call toothache.

Q. What causes tooth decay?
A. A lot of tooth decay is caused by eating foods which have had sugar added to them to make them sweet — chocolate and sweets, cakes and biscuits, ice cream and lollies, fizzy drinks and squash.

After you have eaten something sugary, a sweet sticky layer is left on your teeth. The tiny living things called bacteria, which live in your mouth, start to feed on this layer. They form a sticky substance called plaque on and around your teeth. As the bacteria feed on the sugar, they produce an acid which attacks the hard enamel surface of your teeth.

The acid gradually wears a hole in the enamel. When the acid reaches the dentine, the tooth begins to ache. If the decay reaches the pulp it can be very painful and the infection may sprea

Q. If I get tooth decay, do I have to have the tooth out?
A. If the tooth is very badly decayed, you may have to have it out, but the dentist will try to save it if possible. She will drill out all the rotte part and clean up what is left of the tooth. Then she will fill up the hole, called a cavity, with material that will not decay. In the past, a silver-coloured mixture called amalgam was us for fillings. Today, white-coloured mixtures are often used — especially for front teeth.

Q. Can I stop myself getting tooth decay?
A. Yes, by watching what you eat and by lookin after your teeth properly. The greatest dangers to your teeth are snacks of sweet foods and drinks which you eat between meals. If you only eat sugar in your food at meal-times, you are les likely to get tooth decay.

Q. How often should I brush my teeth?
A. At least twice a day, after breakfast and before you go to bed. Brushing your teeth helps to remove plaque and to keep your gums health It also gets rid of any tiny pieces of food that are stuck between your teeth. So brushing your teet keeps your mouth fresh and stops you from getting bad breath.

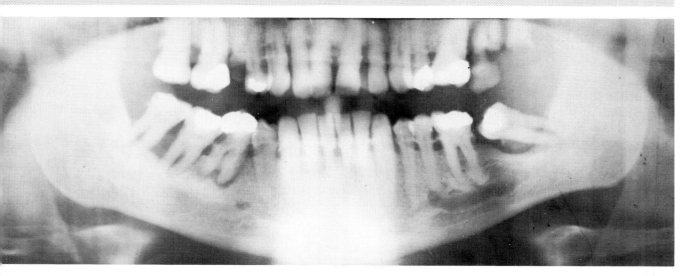

This X-ray shows an unhealthy mouth — there are a lot more fillings, some missing teeth and the loss of bone around teeth suggests bone disease

What sort of toothpaste should I use?
If you use a toothpaste which contains the substance called fluoride, it helps to prevent tooth decay. Fluoride makes the enamel on your teeth stronger, so they are less likely to get damaged by decay.

How often should I go to the dentist?
Once every six months for a check-up. Don't wait until you get toothache. The dentist can spot a tiny hole in a tooth and fill it before it starts to hurt.

How much does it cost to go to the dentist?
A check-up costs you nothing and you can get free treatment until you are 16. But it pays to look after your teeth while you are young, because when you are an adult you have to pay part of the cost of any treatment.

Group work

How much do you know about teeth care? Make up a quiz consisting of ten statements about teeth and teeth care, some of which are true and some of which are false. Write out the questions, but not the answers, then give the test to another group to do. Here is a suggestion for the first question from such a quiz:

A tooth is made mainly of enamel. True or false?

FOR YOUR FOLDER

Work with a partner. In your rough book, list, in order of importance, ten facts about teeth care which you have learned from these pages. Then, compare your list with those which other pairs have made.
Together with the rest of the class, decide what you think are 'The Ten Most Important Facts about Teeth Care'. Ask your teacher to write them on the board, then copy them into your folder.
Your dentist wants to brighten up her waiting room. Draw a poster for her to put up on the wall, giving some advice for people of your age on how to look after your teeth.
Draw a cartoon strip showing EITHER how Charlie Couldn't-Care-Less eats the wrong kinds of snacks, does not look after his teeth properly and ends up at the dentist with toothache and has to have several fillings, OR how Susie Sensible chooses the right kinds of snacks, cleans her teeth carefully, goes for regular check-ups and has no problems with her teeth.

Keep it Clean

Personal check-up

Do you really care for your teeth? Answer the questions and keep a record of the points you score. At the end of the quiz, add up your score and check to see whether or not you are looking after your teeth properly.

1 How often do you eat sweets or chocolate?
2 to 3 times a day   Score 1
once a day   Score 2
once a week   Score 3
less than once a week   Score 4
never   Score 5

2 If you had to choose a snack from these foods, which one would you choose?
a packet of crisps   Score 4
a bar of chocolate   Score 1
an apple   Score 4
a biscuit   Score 1
a piece of cake   Score 1

3 How often do you clean your teeth?
after every meal   Score 5
at least twice a day   Score 4
once a day   Score 3
2 or 3 times a week   Score 2
once a week   Score 1

4 When did you last buy a new toothbrush?
during the last 3 months   Score 5
during the last year   Score 3
over a year ago   Score 1

5 Do you use a flouride toothpaste?
Yes   Score 5
No   Score 2
Don't know   Score 2

6 When did you last go to the dentist for a check-up?
within the last 6 months   Score 5
within the last year   Score 3
over a year ago   Score 1

7 How many fillings have you got?
over 5   Score 1
1 to 5   Score 3
none   Score 5

8 Would you mind if you had to have false teeth?
yes   Score 5
probably   Score 3
no   Score 1

CHECK YOUR SCORE

Below 18   You aren't looking after your teeth properly.
19 to 29   You need to take more care of your teeth than you are doing at present.
30 to 37   You look after your teeth well.
38 to 39   Excellent. You really care for your teeth.

A clean healthy skin is one of the body's best defences against germs.
To keep it clean you should try to wash all over once a day.

DON'T BE A STINKER

When you get hot, excited or do some exercise, your body sweats. The sweat evaporates and you lose heat, so sweating helps your body keep itself at the right temperature. Your body produces about a litre of sweat a day. Sweat consists of water and a small amount of other substances.

Your underarms are likely to sweat quite heavily and when that happens, bacteria (germs) grow. It is the germs mixing with the sweat that cause body odour. So you need to wash under your arms every day to stop the bacteria growing and to get rid of the smell of stale sweat.

A good wash is usually enough to keep you sweet-smelling. But after you have washed with soap and water you may like to use either an antiperspirant (to help stop you sweating heavily) or a deodorant (to help reduce the smell of sweat during the day).

Keep your clothes clean
A clean body will soon get smelly if you don't keep the clothes you're wearing clean too. Try to change the clothes that you wear close to your skin every day:
- underpants
- knickers
- vest
- bra
- tights
- socks

Wash your other clothes as soon as they get dirty or smelly. Clothes made from man-made fibres don't let the perspiration evaporate as easily as cotton, wool, and wool fibres, so you may need to change them more often.

Always wash your hands
Everything you touch is covered with very small, living organisms. Some of these are *bacteria* and *viruses* — 'germs'. Sometimes germs are harmful.

If you have germs on your hands when you eat, the germs can get into your food. This can cause tummy upsets, sickness and diarrhoea. And some germs can cause food poisoning. So of all the parts of your body, your hands need washing most often.

Always make sure you wash your hands:
- before you prepare food or eat it;
- after you go to the toilet;
- whenever they look or feel dirty.

Keep your feet fresh
Damp, sweaty feet smell bad and can also develop skin infections like athlete's foot.

- To keep your feet fresh and healthy, wash them every day and dry them thoroughly afterwards, particularly between the toes.
- Change your socks or tights every day.
- Try to wear socks made from wool, cotton, or mixed fibres like cotton/acrylic. Manmade fibres don't allow your feet to 'breathe' so easily and may make them sweat more.
- Keep your toenails short – you'll find it's more comfortable and they're easier to keep clean. Cut straight across the nail with a small pair of scissors or nail clippers.
- Always wear shoes or boots which fit well. There should be a half-inch gap between the top of your longest toe and the end of your shoe.

FOR YOUR FOLDER

How could you present these ideas on personal hygiene simply, so that younger children could understand them? Design a poster that could be used in a primary school to put across these points.

Care For Your Hair

Why bother?

You should brush and comb your hair regularly every day. Comb your hair thoroughly, especially over the ears and at the back of the neck. Start by combing underneath your hair upwards, then comb it downwards.

It is important to use a suitable comb, which has teeth which are not spaced too far apart. Plastic is a good material for a comb because it is flexible, so the teeth do not break easily. Plastic combs are cheap to buy and easy to clean using a nail brush, washing up liquid and warm water.

Most people prefer to have a brush and comb of their own. But there is no reason why you should not share a brush and comb with other members of your family. You cannot pick up head lice from brushes and combs.

Hair gets dirty very quickly, so you should wash your hair at least once a week. Besides getting rid of the dirt, washing also helps to get rid of grease. There are lots of different shampoo you can use, depending on how greasy your hair gets.

If you get dandruff, you may want to try using a special shampoo. Dandruff is not an illness, it is small flakes of skin from your scalp. Unlike lice, which cling to your hair, dandruff comes off if you wash or brush your hair. Dandruff is unsightly, but it is not harmful. It is nothing to worry about unless you suffer very badly and it makes your scalp sore. If your scalp does become sore, then ask your doctor for advice.

Ten facts about head lice

1 Head lice are very common. One in three children are affected by them at some time.

2 The age group most likely to catch head lice is the 4- to 6-year-old group.

3 Head lice are small, grey insects, which live in hair and feed by sucking blood from the scalp.

4 Nits are the eggs laid by the female louse. They are small, grey and shiny. They cling to the hair until they hatch into lice.

5 Lice cannot jump or fly. The only way they can move is directly from head to head.

6 It used to be thought that getting your hair cut short would protect you against head lice. But lice can live in hair of any length.

7 Lice can live in either clean or dirty hair. Washing your hair does not protect you from lice because lice are protected against water by a layer of wax.

8 Regular brushing or combing of hair helps to protect you against lice. When you comb your hair properly, you can injure any lice that are in it. Once a louse is damaged, it cannot recover.

9 You can get rid of lice by using a lotion, which you can buy from a chemist. You must rub the lotion all over your scalp, and leave it for twelve hours before washing it out.

10 It is easy and simple to treat head lice. The real problem is detecting them. The insects are so small that you can have them for three months but not realise until the bites start to itch.

se the information on the previous page to solve the crossword.

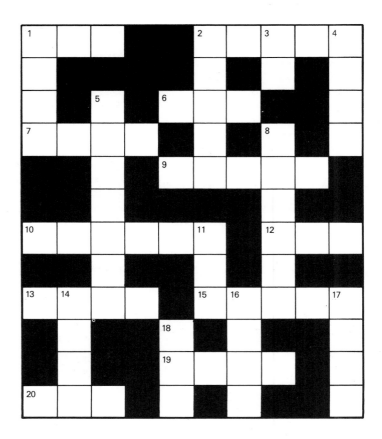

Clues Across

1 Water does not kill lice because they are protected by a layer of this (3)
2 What lice suck from your scalp (5)
6 To get rid of lice you must _____ your hair and scalp thoroughly with 10 across (3)
7 The only way to get rid of lice is to use a chemical that will _____ them (4)
9 People used to think you would not get lice if your hair was this length (5)
10 What a chemist will give you to put on your head to get rid of lice (6)
12 If you need advice about lice you can always _____ your doctor or chemist (3)
13 Lice bite your scalp and eventually cause it to do this (4)
15 The ones in your comb must not be spaced too far apart or they won't injure any lice in your hair (5)
19 Some lice are this colour (4)
20 Lice cannot do this (3)

Clues Down

1 You should wash your hair once a _____ at least (4)
2 People used to think you could pick up lice by sharing one with other members of your family (5)
3 You should check your hair regularly for lice, particularly behind your ears, at the back of your head and _____ your neck (2)
4 Washing your hair gets rid of this (4)
5 Modern combs are usually made of this material (7)
8 Washing your hair helps to get rid of this too (6)
11 The egg laid by a louse (3)
14 If you find you have head lice, you should _____ all your friends (4)
16 You use them to see with, so you should protect them by covering them when you are treating yourself to get rid of head lice (4)
17 What nits cling to on your head (4)
18 What a nit is (3)

What Is There To Do?

What do *you* do in your free time?

Each weekday during term time you get between four and five hours a day of free time. At the weekend you get another twenty hours or so.

Some of your free time will have to be spent doing homework, so what do you spend your time doing? Have you enough time to do everything you want? Do you get bored?

FOR YOUR FOLDER

On a piece of paper write down an estimate of how many hours each week of your free time you think you spend on different types of activity. Put the list in your folder, then carry out a 'free time check' to see how accurate your estimate was.

At the end of the week, work out how much time you spent on each activity. Then, draw either a pie-chart or a bar graph showing the results of your time-check — like the bar graph showing how Tina spent her weekend. Compare how much time you actually spent on each activity with the estimate you made before you did your time-check. How accurate was your estimate?

Class discussion

On a large chart, write down how much time each member of the class spent on each of the activities during the week you kept your free time check.

What conclusions can you draw from your survey about how the people in your class spend their free time?

As your results will probably show, a great deal of your leisure-time is spent watching TV. Organise a class debate on the motion: 'This house believes that children aged 11 and 12 spend too much time watching TV.' Ask for volunteers to propose and oppose the motion, and for people to second them. Give them time to prepare their speeches, and then hold the debate. At the end of the debate take a vote to see whether the motion is passed.

Sunday.

9-10   tidied bedroom /Did homework
10-11 took dog for a walk
11-12 listened to records
1-5   went out to see Gran
5-6   watched TV
7-8   watched TV
8-9   read my book

MY WEEKEND

Saturday.

9-10   stayed in bed reading
10-12 went roller-skating
12-1   helped get lunch (chores!)
2-4   went round to a friends
4-5   took dog for walk
5-6   watched TV
7-10   watched TV

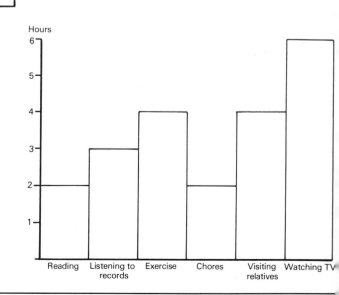

Where can we go?

BRIXTON RECREATION CENTRE
Brixton Station Road, Brixton SW9 8QQ
01-274 7774

REGAL CINEMA ABINGDON
PHONE 20322
NOW SHOWING (AFTERNOONS ONLY)
RETURN TO OZ (U)
Afternoons at 2pm, Thursday, Friday, Saturday
Also showing Sunday 3rd at 3pm
STARTING FRIDAY NOVEMBER 1ST FOR SEVEN DAYS
(Evenings only)
CLINT EAST...
(15)
OPEN 7 NIGHTS

OXFORD ICE SKATING
OXIST
Responsible for or...
individ...
Sessions — Sun...
New members welco...

COLNE VALLEY RIDING CENTRE
Large indoor

ACTON BATHS
Children's Fun Sessions
Inflatables
Swimming lessons
Toys etc.
Life-saving courses

In pairs

Work with a partner and carry out an investigation into the leisure facilities that are provided in your area.

Collect general information. Find out from the library, the local council offices or the Citizens Advice Bureau about the leisure and recreational facilities provided by your local council.
Look in local newspapers and contact your local Tourist Information Office to find out what's on locally and what other entertainment facilities there are.

Carry out a detailed study.
a) Choose one of the leisure facilities provided in your area and visit it to make a detailed study.
b) Before your visit, make a list of all the basic information about it which you want to find out, e.g. opening times, entrance charges, details of activities and facilities provided, any special features.
c) Make a list of questions to ask yourself about the service it provides, such as:
  Is it easy to get to by public transport?
  Is it an attractive place — well-decorated and in good repair?
  Does it make special provisions for the unemployed, the old and the handicapped?
  If there are entrance charges, do you think they are too high or about right?
  Are there any facilities which it does not provide, but which you think it should?
  Do you get the impression that the facility is well-used or under-used?
d) Interview a number of people who are using the facility. Draw up a list of questions to ask them about their views, such as:
  How often do you come here?
  Have you travelled far in order to come here?
  Are you satisfied with the facilities here?
  Do you think the facilities could be improved, and if so how?

3 Present a report. Tell the rest of the class what you found out during your detailed study. You could present your findings in the form of a written article, like a newspaper article; you could give a talk or you could invite the class to interview you and ask you questions about what you found out.

FOR YOUR FOLDER
Imagine that a pen-friend is coming to spend a week's holiday with you. Write to her or him explaining what leisure facilities there are in your area and suggesting how you could spend your time together.

Play Safe

The Blue Code

It's fun to play in or near water. But every year fun turns to tragedy for some children. Water is dangerous, unless you take care and act responsibly. The Royal Life Saving Society issues guidelines for water safety known as the Blue Code. Whenever you play in or near water, observe the Blue Code.

In pairs

Study the details of the Blue Code. Go through the points to remember one by one and suggest the reasons for each piece of advice.
Work out a test consisting of fifteen questions on the Blue Code. Then, join up with another pair and give your test to them to do — without looking at the code! See which of you can get the highest marks on the other's test.

1. Swimming

* Never swim alone or when tired
* Wait at least an hour after a meal before swimming
* Don't show off
* Cold water can kill - get out as soon as you feel cold
* Take the advice of the lifeguards
* Don't take airbeds and inflatable toys into the sea
* At the seaside, check tide tables and ask what the local dangers are
* Swim in line with the shore
* Don't dive into unknown waters
* Don't wear goggles to dive other than when doing a racing dive
* If you need to wear goggles look for the kite mark

2. On the water

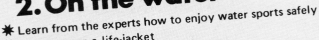

* Learn from the experts how to enjoy water sports safely
* Always wear a life-jacket
* Keep equipment in good working order
* Tell someone where you are going and when you will be back
* When boating wear warm clothing and non-slip footwear
* Never canoe alone
* Don't overload a boat
* Learn and Practise the capsize and man overboard drills
* Stay with a capsized boat

3. Out and about

* Report lifesaving equipment you see missing or anyone taking or breaking it
* Read and obey notices and never cover them up
* Keep away from disused gravel pits and quarries
* Watch out for slippery and crumbling river banks
* Never fish alone
* Keep a watchful eye on toddlers near water
* Keep off ice covered ponds, lakes or canals

n groups

Emergency

In groups of three, act out a conversation in which a person makes an emergency call to the police or coastguard. Take it in turns to be the person reporting the emergency, the operator and either the police officer or the coastguard. Before you begin, decide what the emergency is and study the 999 drill.

FOR YOUR FOLDER

Draw a series of pictures to illustrate the advice you are given about swimming in the Blue Code. Write a caption for each picture. Draw a poster to warn young children of junior school age about the dangers of playing near water.

4. If you fall in

* Keep calm
* Call for help
* Float on your back
* To attract attention wave one arm only

5. If someone else falls in

DON'T GO IN THE WATER

* Look for something to help pull him out (stick, rope, scarf), lie down so that you will not be pulled in too.
* If you cannot reach him, throw any floating object (rubber ring or ball) for him to hold on to, then FETCH HELP.

6. At home

* Watch toddlers at all times
* Cover fish ponds and pools with mesh
* Keep baths empty and bath plugs out of reach of small children
* Empty paddling pools when not in use

7. The 999 drill

You do **not** need coins to make an emergency call. The operator will answer a 999 call and ask:-

* 1. Which service you require
* 2. Your telephone number

You should ask for the **Police** (or the **Coastguard** if near the coast) The Police or Coastguard will then ask you:-

* 1. What the trouble is
* 2. Where it is
* 3. Whether anyone is capable of taking action while help is arriving
* 4. The telephone number you are speaking from
* 5. Your name and address

That Was the First Year, That Was

How have you got on?

The aim of this unit is to help you to think about how well you have been doing during your first year and whether you are getting as much out of school as you could be. It is important, therefore, to be honest about yourself. Don't write down anything just because you think that is how you *should* behave or what you *should* think. Write down how you actually do behave and what you actually do think.

Read through these statements about life at school. Choose the statement from each of the groups that applies to you and write it down. The aim is for you to think about what school offers and whether you are making the most of the opportunities it offers you. So there is no scoring scheme for you to check to see how well you have done. Instead, when you have finished, work with a friend. Show her or him what you have written about yourself and talk about what school offers and your attitudes towards school.

1 **Punctuality**
   A I don't worry if I'm late for registration.
   B I'm always there on time for registration.
   C I'm sometimes late for registration, but I try not to be.
   D Sometimes, I'm so late that I miss registration completely.

2 **Attendance**
   A I like school, so I never miss it unless I'm ill.
   B I don't mind coming to school, so I never miss it except for a reason.
   C I don't see why you should have to come to school, so I sometimes don't.
   D I only come to school because you get into trouble if you don't.

3 **Lessons**
   A I think most of the lessons are boring, so I don't pay much attention.
   B I'm interested in most things, so I enjoy all the lessons.
   C Some subjects are better than others, but I always pay attention because I want to do well.
   D I muck about in some lessons, but I try hard in others.

4 **Homework**
   A I hate doing homework, so I don't always do it.
   B I usually enjoy doing my homework.
   C I only do my homework because my Mum/Dad makes me.
   D I always do my homework, but I do it as quickly as possible.

5 **Library**
   A I go to the library about once a week to change my reading book.
   B I don't like reading, so I don't go to the library very often.
   C I only go to the library if I get stuck with my homework.
   D I often go to the library to check facts for my project and to find information for my homework.

6 **Behaviour**
   A I've only been in trouble for my behaviour once or twice this year.
   B I've been in trouble several times for mucking about in lessons.
   C I've been in trouble several times for behaving badly in breaks and in the lunch-hour.
   D I haven't really been in any trouble this year.

7 **Breaktimes and lunch-hours**
   A I never do anything special. I just wander about.
   B I spend the time with my friends either chatting or playing.
   C I sometimes go to a club or a practice, otherwise I spend the time with my friends.
   D I try to find somewhere quiet where I can read or do my homework.

8 **Friendships**
   A I've made at least two new close friends since the beginning of the year.
   B I've made one new close friend since the beginning of the year.

C I don't really have any close friends at school.

D The only friends I've got at school are those I knew before I started this school.

9 **Clubs**

A I haven't bothered to join any school clubs.

B I joined a school club but I only went to one or two meetings.

C I've joined a school club, but I only go when I feel like it.

D I'm in a school club and I go to all the meetings.

10 **Sports and games**

A I'm not much good at games, but I try in lessons.

B I've been in one of the school teams and I always go to practices.

C I could have been in a school team but I didn't want to give up my time.

D I don't like games, so I try to get out of it as much as I can.

11 **Plays and musical events**

A There hasn't been a chance for me to be in a play or a musical event yet, but I would like to be involved in one.

B I'm not interested in plays and musical events.

C I've taken part in at least one performance at school this year.

D I belong to a group outside school that puts on performances, so I don't take part in the school ones.

12 **Trips and outings**

A I prefer to go on trips and outings with just my family or my close friends.

B I've been on at least one trip or outing with the school this year.

C None of the trips or outings interested me, so I haven't been on one.

D I'd like to go on some of the trips and outings, but they are usually too expensive.

FOR YOUR FOLDER

Write your own end-of-year report.

1 Make a list of all the subjects you have been studying. Then, use a five-star system to give yourself grades for, a) Effort — the effort you have put into your work in that subject, and b) Progress — the progress you have made in that subject. (Note: Whether you have come at the top or at the bottom of the class in that subject is not the point. The question you have to ask yourself is: Have *I* made progress?)

2 Now, think about each subject in turn and write at least two or three sentences about your work and progress in that subject.

- Think about what skills you have learned in that subject and what you have managed to achieve.
- Think about what you have found difficult in that subject. How are you going to try to improve your work in that subject next year?

3 Now write a general comment in which you sum up how you feel about your first year. Ask yourself these questions:

Do you think you have settled in well?
Do you think you have worked as hard as you could have worked in lessons?
Have you done your homework well?
Are you well-organised in your approach to school and schoolwork?
Have you got involved in tutor group activities or have you taken a back seat?
Have you joined in the life of the school as fully as possible?
In which areas of the school's life have you made the greatest contribution?
Has your behaviour in, a) lessons, and b) around the school been good?
In what ways do you feel you have changed and grown up during the year?

Before you write your summary, find the envelope in which you wrote your New Year resolutions about schoolwork. Open it. Have you managed to keep your resolutions?

Looking Forward

First year reflections, second year hopes

> Alderman Lee School
> Beckworth
> BKM9 6QF
> 6th July 1985
>
> Dear Mrs. Rogers
> When I first arrived at Alderman Lee, I was worried that
> I might get lost, because it is so much bigger than
> Thurston Primary School. But I soon found my way around
> and I think I have settled in well. I like having to
> carry all my books around more than keeping them in
> a drawer, because you can look through your books and
> see how well you have done during the year.
> On the whole, I got a good report and I enjoyed starting
> new subjects like science and C.D.T. In C.D.T. I
> designed and made a wooden toy for my brother Mark
> and was given a commendation for it. I don't like French,
> though, because I find it rather difficult.
> Some of my teachers said they think I could try harder and
> that I chatter too much. I expect that surprises you. But I
> have changed quite a bit. I'm not nearly as shy as I used
> to be and I've made several new friends.
> I haven't been in much trouble during the year. I've been
> told off a few times for running in the corridors and
> I did get a lunch-time detention for chewing gum in
> class.
> I'm looking forward to being a second year. I want to try to
> get a part in the lower school musical. I wasn't in it this year,
> but I wish I had been. Also, I'm going to try to concentrate
> more in class, especially in French and Maths, because they
> are my weakest subjects.
> Yours sincerely,
>
> Tracy Masters

FOR YOUR FOLDER

Have you enjoyed your first year?
Are you looking forward to the second year?
How will the second year be different from the first year?
What do you hope to achieve during the second year?
Work with a partner and talk about these questions. Each draw up a list of what you are going to concentrate on trying to do during the second year. Call it 'My Targets for my Second Year.'

This letter was written by a comprehensive school pupil to her primary school teacher at the end of her first year at secondary school. Read it, then write a similar letter to your primary school teacher telling her all about your first year at secondary school and what you hope to achieve during the second year.